D1524002

Literary Criticism & the Structures of History

Erich Auerbach & Leo Spitzer

by
Geoffrey Green
Foreword
by
Robert Scholes

University
of
Nebraska Press
Lincoln &
London

Wingate College Library

Copyright 1982 by the University of Nebraska Press
All rights reserved
Manufactured in the United States of America

The paper in this book meets the guidelines for
permanence and durability of the Committee
on Production Guidelines for Book Longevity
of the Council on Library Resources.

Library of Congress Cataloging in Publication Data

Green, Geoffrey, 1951-
Literary criticism and the structures of history,
Erich Auerbach and Leo Spitzer.

Half title: Literary criticism and
the structures of history.
Includes bibliographical references and index.
1. Auerbach, Erich, 1892-1957.   2. Spitzer, Leo,
1887-1960.   I. Title.
PN75.A9G74   801'.95'0922   82-2654
ISBN 0-8032-2108-8   AACR2

To Marcia

DIR 2·13·90 1895

Contents

ix Forward

1 Introduction

9 Acknowledgments

11 Erich Auerbach

83 Leo Spitzer

161 Conclusion

167 Notes

181 Index

Foreword

This is a book a little outside the academic norm. The myths of academic objectivity—"disinterest" in the Arnoldian sense—die hard, as do the myths about the total separation of critical and creative writing. Yet Geoffrey Green has had the temerity to study two scholar-critics as if they were simply writers—men of letters caught up in history and to a great extent the products of it. He shows us in this unusual study how Erich Auerbach's and Leo Spitzer's major contributions to literary study are linked to their personal histories and the larger history of their times, which made them both exiles from their homelands and the academic environments that might have nurtured them more easily but with less stimulation.

Not that Green's study is largely concerned with biographical detail. It isn't. It is a work of interpretation, devoted to the major critical texts of Auerbach and Spitzer, reading them in the light of the personal and historical circumstances from which they emerged. Auerbach's *Mimesis*, for instance, the most influential single work produced by either writer, is interpreted by Green in the context of German discussions of the relationship between Judaism and Christianity, illustrated by excerpts from a sermon preached by Cardinal Faulhaber at Munich in 1933. Similarly, in interpeting Spitzer's work, Green traces the persistent strains of mysticism, combined with a comfortable sense of self-worth, that make the fundamental procedures of Spitzer's critical practice more of a personal mode and less of an adaptable methodology than is usually acknowledged.

An investigation into the careers of these two distinguished exiles is not simply a case of criticism scrutinizing itself, however, for Auerbach and Spitzer were more than literary critics. They were humanists with an abiding concern for the ways in which humanistic study might contribute to culture. There is a powerful ethical strain in their work, which marks them—along with their prodigious learning—as scholars of another time and place. Green's major achievement in this study is the tracing of this ethical strain in each career, the isolation of the special quality in each man's work, and the situation of this individuality in relation to the historical moment that shaped it.

The men, the moment, the milieu—this is a traditional study in its methodology. Only the subject matter is unusual: the treatment of scholars, of philologists, as "writers." But writers they were, because they have had and continue to have readers, and their influence in their adopted country has been strongly felt. It is time for this influence to be better understood. Geoffrey Green's serious and insightful pioneering study constitutes an excellent beginning on this task.

ROBERT SCHOLES

Introduction

"If it be now, 'tis not to come; if it be not to come,
it will be now; if it be not now, yet it will come:
the readiness is all."

    Hamlet (Act 5, Scene 2)

"Look beyond the shadowy scope of time, and, living once
for all in eternity … find the perfect future in the present."

    Nathaniel Hawthorne, "The Birthmark" (1843)

Erich Auerbach and Leo Spitzer were two members of a distinguished German quartet of modern scholars who specialized
in Romance philology. Along with Karl Vossler and Ernst Robert
Curtius, they were the principal practitioners of German Romance
philology, a discipline "inaugurated by Uhland and Diez," and
"rooted in German historicism, a movement whose successive pro-
ponents from Herder to the Schlegels and Jacob Grimm, were com-
mitted to the idea of an historical development manifested in the
individual *Volksgeist*."[1] As a group, the four exerted a significant
influence on European literary studies. But in response to nazism,
both Auerbach and Spitzer emigrated to the United States. Their
presence enriched the American critical environment and helped
change the way we think about literature, literary criticism, and the
historical process.

    Auerbach and Spitzer adhered to an expansive conception of

1

philology as the premier branch of scholarship embracing all historical fields of knowledge. Whereas philosophy considers the nature of
laws that are timeless and everlasting, philology has as its terrain the
conditional and particular aspects of historical reality. In this, they
carried on Vico's distinction: "Philosophy contemplates reason,
whence comes knowledge of the true; philology observes that of
which human choice is author, whence comes consciousness of the
certain."[2]

Their intellectual tradition had its roots in German historicism,
which, according to Auerbach, emanated "from the so-called Storm
and Stress group of the 1770's, from the first works of Herder and
Goethe and their friends; later from the Schlegel brothers and the
other German romanticists"; historicism is "the conviction that every
civilization and every period has its own possibilities of aesthetic
perfection; that the works of art of the different peoples and periods,
as well as their general forms of life, must be understood as products
of variable individual conditions, and have to be judged each by his
own development, not by absolute rules of beauty and ugliness."[3]

Another influence on both scholars—closely related to German
historicism and developing as well from Romanticism—is the tradition of *Geistesgeschichte* ("history of spirit"). The term *Geist*, according
to Spitzer, includes *"all* the creative impulses of the human mind
(e.g., feelings)." It emphasizes synthesis over analysis and centers on
the principle that "an idea [is not] detachable from the soul of the man
who begot or received the idea [or] from the spiritual climate which
nourished it." *Geistesgeschichte* focuses on "the totality of the features
of a given period or movement which the historian tries to *see as a
unity*—and the impact of which ... does in fact amount to more than
that of the aggregate of the parts." Jakob Burckhardt, Wilhelm Dilthey, Georg Simmel, Max Weber, Ernst Troeltsch were all, in
Spitzer's view, noted exponents of *Geistesgeschichte*.[4]

The tradition of *Geistesgeschichte* encourages the historian to find
an integral concordance among the artistic, cultural, scientific, and
historical realms of man's activities. Such an enterprise echoes Vico's

call for "the ideal history of the eternal laws which are instanced by the deeds of all nations" rather than "the particular history in time of the laws and deeds" of any one nation. Vico's emphasis on an "ideal eternal history" based on the "natural law" and history of "the peoples," as well as his insistence on a "universal republic of letters" led many adherents of historicistic *Geistesgeschichte* (including Auerbach and Spitzer) to recognize Vico as an important ancestor predating its roots in German Romanticism. According to Isaiah Berlin, Vico "uncovered a species of knowing not previously clearly discriminated, the embryo that later grew into the ambitious and luxuriant plant of German historicist *Verstehen*—empathic insight, intuitive sympathy, historical *Einfühlung*, and the like."[5]

The common intellectual background shared by the four men did not prevent a change in approach that occurred as a result of the advent of Hitlerism. Auerbach and Spitzer—themselves in movement from Germany to Istanbul to the United States—embraced the principles of *becoming* over *being*: literary history was an evolutionary process in time. Vossler (1872–1949) and Curtius, remaining in Germany, emphasized the fixed and timeless nature of literature; in Curtius's words, "continuity became more important to me than actuality." He noted that "we no longer feel it incumbent on us to justify the ways of God to man."[6]

A brief examination of the career of Curtius (1886–1956) will help provide clarification of the divergence among the four scholars. The Alsace locality of his birth with its Franco-Germanic culture offered him an early experience of Europe that transcended nationalistic values. Although trained as a medievalist under the instruction of Gustav Gröber (whose positivistic and historicistic concerns helped pioneer the conception of Romance philology in the twentieth century), Curtius achieved his initial reputation as an authority on European modernist literature: his engaging essays contained original interpretations of modernistic literary works at a time when few readers were able to comprehend their operational principles. Knowledgeable about contemporary philosophical trends, and maintaining personal acquaintances with many of the notable literary figures of the period, Curtius was viewed as a literary critic whose explications of the works of particular authors of various nationalities were meant to help engender a pan-European humanistic atmosphere.

The social and political disruption in Germany prompted Curtius to produce a remonstrative tract against what he believed were the self-destructive and antihumanistic tendencies of the German culture (*Deutscher Geist in Gefahr*, 1932). But with the outbreak of war, Curtius returned to the past and his philological training; throughout the war, he researched the Latin literature of the Middle Ages. The result, *European Literature and the Latin Middle Ages* (1948) is one of the seminal works of literary scholarship in our time. He investigated *topoi* (the designs of order in antiquity that were incorporated—with the breakdown of social and cultural denominations—into language as rhetorical functions and appeared in literature as stock formulations). Curtius utilized *topoi* in an effort to establish the continuity of European culture and literature from antiquity to the present age. With the world again at peace, Curtius's work was applauded by nations who—although previously antagonistic—were ardent for affirmation of a universal humanism.

Curtius emphasized the degree to which his own work, like the development of the literature he studied, remained thematically coherent. "Life," he believed, ". . . goes beyond itself in order to participate in something that is no longer life."[7] Thus, his writing was unified by his conception of the process of literary evolution as hermetic and irremovable, changeless and eternal—"something that is no longer life." Such a vantage point stresses what prevails: Curtius's lifelong advocacy of a Europe united by its common literary antecedents and by those placid and enduring humanistic values that dominated its civilization.

Diminished by this approach of stability is the sense of man's existence as a historical drama: the manner in which life stands before us in all of its immediacy as a perpetual process of present

4

occurrence. From this motile perspective, man and his literature are subsumed in the emergent dynamic of historical change. Curtius's work would be depicted (in the words of Benedetto Croce) as one man's "act of comprehending and understanding induced by the requirements of practical life."[8] Such a mode of analysis in regard to Curtius makes several allusions possible. His Alsatian origins may have wielded an effect on his commitment to the unity of the French and German cultures. Modernism may have exerted an appeal for Curtius because his sensibility was resistant to nationalism and its boundaries. The Nazi regime in Germany and the European war may have represented, for Curtius, the demolition of his harmonic ideals. Finally, it is possible that Curtius's return to the Middle Ages as a subject for inquiry constituted an attempt at denial of the violent and destructive world at war—a denial that was transformed by the resumption of peace into the most sublime sagacity.

While Curtius and Vossler, under the duress of history, sought as their goal the determination of an aloof and absolute truth, Auerbach and Spitzer, also in response to history, strove to attain that literary process which would realize, in Américo Castro's words, "a form of conversation, a living companionship with those who in one way or another have left behind them a living expression of their lives. . . . The historian . . . confronts lives that are in the process of *doing*, that are trying to communicate with, or obtain something from, other lives."[9]

It was for this reason that Auerbach and Spitzer reminded Curtius of his fruitful presence in Germany during the Second World War. Similarly, Spitzer, in criticizing Vossler's interpretation of Jewish themes in sixteenth-century literature, included this rebuke: "But should [Vossler] not have forgotten his clever transitions, when faced with the plight of Israel in the Germany (his Germany) of 1938, a situation no less critical than that of 1553?"[10]

These were scholars whose works of literary criticism were aroused and stimulated by the structures of historical change. But for Auerbach and Spitzer, this interaction with history attuned them in an

5

extraordinary way to the manner in which literature and history are profoundly interrelated. Auerbach's account of their experience is signal: "The most priceless and indispensable part of a philologist's heritage is still his own nation's culture and language. Only when he is first separated from this heritage, however, and then transcends it does it become truly effective. We must return . . . to . . . the knowledge that the spirit [*Geist*] is not national."[11]

As writers-in-exile, Auerbach and Spitzer existed in a world of cross-culturation; they functioned in a context of transformation. They were compelled to reckon with their own artistic and intellectual antecedents, with the cultural migration they were experiencing. They created works of literary criticism that situated themselves in the most complex and torrid regions where societies confront each other, fictions merge with societies, conceptions become actions, and images become words. They unceasingly attempted to probe the nature of their identities as authors, the validity of their critical tradition in exile, and the essential conceptual space that existed for a writer who was striving for nothing less than to imprint the mores of his artist's individual creative society on the collective society-at-large.

Both Auerbach and Spitzer were literary critics and historians. From their distinctive perspectives, they aggressively sought to formulate a configuration for literature that would be in accordance with the dynamics of history. As a result of their emigration from Europe to the United States, they drew on the traditions and intellectual resources of two historical cultures in order to investigate the properties of Western literary evolution. Thus, to consider their work is to encounter again the literary and historical past that forms the basis for all present inquiry.

Each man conceived his task as the creation of immediate expressions about what is past, or passing, or to come. That body of criticism, enveloped in immediacy, has become frozen in a doctrinaire past: their work has never been evaluated according to their individual estimation of it. One approach toward reappraising the work of Auerbach and Spitzer is to focus on their own emphasis on historical process and change. Historical relativism amid the contingencies of spiritual continuity, historical and linguistic evolution, generic development and alteration, historical and literary structure: these persistent themes serve to underline that aspect of movement and flux which characterized both men's careers—namely, cultural migration during a time of historical and social crisis. As authors and critics, they were concerned with literature, but outside those roles, they could not (nor did they wish to) confine their criticism to literary texts; their interests extended to politics, religion, history, ideology. Their work must be returned to the context and climate of its composition. Only then, with a resuscitated sense of their historical intentionality, can the process of our own assessment be undertaken.

The following pages will, I hope, help to illuminate the concerns and priorities, both literary and historical, of Erich Auerbach and Leo Spitzer, which are at the center of our own intellectual pursuits.

Acknowledgments

The idea for this study originated with one portion of my doctoral dissertation. I appreciate the help of the American Council of Learned Societies whose grant-in-aid enabled me to undertake new research that developed and expanded the original idea into the present volume. The following individuals read all or part of the manuscript and contributed valuable suggestions: Jackson I. Cope, Leslie A. Fiedler, René Girard, Frank Kermode, Marcus Klein, and Marjorie Perloff. I would like to thank all those friends whose spirited conversation on a variety of topics helped me to refine my thoughts on literary criticism and the historical process.

I owe a different sort of debt to my parents for their constant encouragement and love. I am obliged to all my family for their warmth and fellowship. Finally, I am grateful to my wife, Marcia, who is always there for me. Her presence makes everything possible.

Erich Auerbach

When Erich Auerbach died in 1957, the world lost a distinguished scholar. Many academic journals mourned his passing; they referred to his impressive contributions in Romance philology, and to his expertise in medieval studies, Latin antiquity, and Christian symbolism. The implication was that a venerable elder statesman had passed away, a man whose literary output had long been completed. But at his death Auerbach was a man of only sixty-four years. He had not begun to write until he was thirty-seven. He had been actively immersed in new projects, studies, and deliberations.

With the passing years, his critical stature increased. He was cited as one of the greatest literary scholars of the century, one of a remarkable group of brilliant German scholars—Karl Vossler, E. R. Curtius, and Leo Spitzer—all of whom had concentrated on Romance philology.[1] Central to all assessments of Auerbach, however, was the notion of the particular isolated quality of his investigations: he had completed several important and intricate textual explications of Dante; he had explored the development of realism as it evolved through various literary periods; and he had clarified the conception of Christian figural interpretation, demonstrating its influence during the medieval period.

But never has his work been evaluated according to his own estimation of it: "My purpose is always to write history." His studies have never been considered according to the unifying principles Auerbach had in mind. Comparing his work to that of Vossler, Curtius, and Spitzer, he wrote:

11

My work, however, shows a much clearer awareness of the European crisis. At an early date, and from then on with increasing urgency, I ceased to look upon the European possibilities of Romance philology as mere possibilities and came to regard them as a task specific to our time—a task which could not have been envisaged yesterday and will no longer be conceivable tomorrow. European civilization is approaching the term of its existence; its history as a distinct entity would seem to be at an end. [2]

The reasons for the difficulty in assessing Auerbach according to a functional context are contained in his work. Although his purpose was to write history, he believed that "today it is no longer possible to represent the history of our life style, that is, the history of the last three thousand years, as a process governed by laws." Yet he urgently believed in the European crisis and wished to "attempt to form a lucid and coherent picture of this civilization and its unity." His method of achieving that picture was "to select, develop, and correlate strictly limited and readily accessible problems in such a way that they will operate as keys to the whole." But that whole "can never be expressed in abstract or extrahistorical terms, but only as a dialectical, dramatic process." Any truths to be gained, then, from the explication of specific texts must be evaluated and appreciated in a historically relative manner. There is a limit to our objective understanding of our lives and histories because we are currently alive and in history. Such "radical historical relativism," as Auerbach termed it, was derived from his study of the laws of Giambattista Vico. [3]

Auerbach provides, in the methodological section of his *Literary Language and Its Public in Late Latin Antiquity and in the Middle Ages* (from which I have derived much of the material for this initial discussion of his critical method), a mature statement of his relative historic method:

The general conception that can be set forth is, I believe, that of an historical process, a kind of drama, which advances no theory but only sketches a certain pattern of human destiny. The subject of this drama is Europe; I have tried to approach this subject in a number of partial investigations. What can thus be achieved under the most favorable circumstances is an insight into the diverse implications of a process from which we stem and in which we participate, a definition of our present situation and also perhaps of the possibilities for the immediate future. In any event, such a method compels us to look within ourselves and to set forth our consciousness of ourselves here and now, in all its wealth and limitations.

Has such an approach scientific validity? It matters little. [Pp. 21–22]

The fine distinction here between the theory that Auerbach eschews and the historical pattern he advocates begins to break down when we are faced with a pattern that enables us to gain insight into, and perhaps foresee, the course of the future.

Other problematic elements in this passage are Auerbach's insistence on "partial investigations," and the ambiguous meaning of "to look within ourselves and to set forth our consciousness of ourselves here and now." We can see the first element as being part of that reluctance to express anything absolutely, or ahistorically: it must always be appreciated from within a historical, perspectivistic process. But the second element is more elusive. The interior soul-searching reflects a kind of mystical humanism that would seem odd within the radical relativistic framework. Granting the subjective quality of our perceptions about life, how are we to reach anything but a tentative grasp of our interior consciousness? What the passage reveals is an extreme reticence to propose analytical and descriptive truths about mankind; yet we can also perceive the desire to be able to rely ultimately on something, the impulse to attempt certain kinds of predictions.

When faced with such perplexing aspects, it is not surprising that critics and scholars chose to avoid any active attempt to elucidate Auerbach's work in terms of the framework in which he conceived it. Indeed, although Auerbach called on his readers to "sense the unity behind" the fragmented studies (p. 24), such a search is by no means simple to undertake. It was more satisfying to rely on the precision and profundity of Auerbach's minute and contextual observations.

And such was the brilliance of Auerbach's work that there seemed to be no end to the fascinating particular insights and explanations.

Again and again, however, Auerbach provided evidence that he wished his works to be accepted as full-scale all-encompassing sociological depictions of the historical societies that provided the contexts for the specific literary texts he was examining. His method, he wrote, "consists in finding unusually fertile areas or key problems on which it is rewarding to concentrate, because they open up a knowledge of a broader context and cast a light on entire historical landscapes" (p. 18).

For Auerbach, one aspect of the logical movement from literary fragment to relativistic historical insight was provided by Vico's theory of knowledge, which Auerbach embraced. The key point is Vico's

equation of the historical with the human. For him the world of the nations . . . embraces not only political history but also the history of thought, of expression (language, literature, the fine arts), religion, law, and economics. Because all these follow from the cultural state of human society in a given period and consequently must be understood in relation to one another or else cannot be understood at all, an insight into one of these facets of human creativity at a given stage of development must provide a key to all the others at the same stage.[4]

The linking of the historical with the human enabled Auerbach to remain within the relativistic historical mode of analysis he admired and still strive for larger cultural and sociological connections. But if one aspect of society must be understood in relation to another (or else, not at all), the key that the understanding of the one element provides is rather nebulous unless, at some ultimate point, there is an absolute: a notion upon which the relatives can begin to accumulate constructively.

As we shall see, Auerbach was proceeding from certain valued concepts which, far from being detached and relativistic for him, were urgently important and ideologically crucial. Instead of gaining insight into our collective participation in history, Auerbach attempted to outline the path of past history and then to use his version of history as a fortress—an arsenal—from which he could wage a passionate and vehement war against the possible flow of history in his time.

Auerbach perceived that it was not easy, within an extreme relativistic framework, to obtain any reliable insight into human creativity at a specific stage of evolution. It was harder still, he realized, to move from particular insight into larger knowledge. He attempted to clarify the problem:

Our historic way of feeling and judging is so deeply rooted in us that we have ceased to be aware of it. . . . It is true that perspectivistic understanding fails as soon as political interests are at stake; but otherwise, especially in aesthetic matters, our historic capacity for adaptation to the most various forms of beauty is almost boundless. . . .

It is wrong to believe that historical relativism or perspectivism makes us incapable of evaluating and judging the work of art, that it leads to arbitrary eclecticism, and that we need, for judgement, fixed and absolute categories. . . . Each historian (we may also call him, with Vico's terminology, "philologist") has to undertake this task for himself, since historical relativism has a twofold aspect: it concerns the understanding historian as well as the phenomena to be understood. This is an extreme relativism; but we should not fear it. . . . The historian does not become incapable of judging; he learns what judging means. Indeed, he will soon cease to search for such categories of judgement. The general human quality, common to the most perfect works of the particular periods, which alone may provide for such categories, can be grasped only in its particular forms, or else as a dialectical process in history; its abstract essence cannot be expressed in exact significant terms. It is from the material itself that he will learn to extract the categories or concepts which he needs for describing and distinguishing the different phenomena. These concepts are not absolute; they are elastic and provisional, changeable with changing history. But they will be sufficient to enable us to discover what the different phenomena mean within their own period, and what they mean within the three thousand years of conscious literary human life we know of; and finally, what they mean to us, here and now. That is judgement enough.[5]

What emerges from this is, first of all, Auerbach's affirmation that, as a philologist, he is a historian; he means his studies to exist within and comment on a historical frame. And all of us are so steeped in history that our judgments are historically influenced even when we are not conscious of this connection. But then Auerbach admits that our relativistic understanding fails when political affinities are involved. Such a contradiction creates a difficulty, for how (according to the earlier quotation) can political history exist in a sphere apart from aesthetic matters? Since Auerbach claims that both of these are related to each other in terms of our analysis and comprehension of them, and since we must place them in relation or not understand them at all, how can we maintain a perspectivistic understanding about aesthetic matters, but not about political ones?

The historian must learn to judge by unhistorical categories. It is the "general human quality" that is "common to the most perfect works of the particular periods" that inspires us to search for our absolute modes of evaluation, but it is only possible to discern that human quality through the particular and volatile historical form. We lack the terms to express the "abstract essence" of the general human quality. By evaluating the human quality within each historical context and specific literary work, particular and relative concepts and modes of analysis will emerge. These concepts are tentative; they vary from historical milieu to milieu. They are valid within their own historical period. How do they enable us to understand each period from the perspective of three thousand years of literary history—a history composed of actively varying milieus and relativistic concepts?

Ultimately, Auerbach proposed that each particular period in the flow of history has its own relative and specialized qualities. Since history is an ongoing process, we can only relate to the qualities of each period from within the relativistic context of its historical perspective. Analyzing the cultural aspects of each period will provide partial insights into the nature of each age: "If we assume with Vico that every age has its characteristic unity, every text must provide a partial view on the basis of which a synthesis is possible."[6]

But in every age and within every varying period, great literary works will be created. These, of course, will differ because they are dynamically related to the institutions and the ideas of their historical age. In the "most perfect" of these works in every period, however, a general human quality will emerge. These qualities serve as keys to the characteristic unity of each age. Since every period produces works that are most perfect, and since in every most perfect work one can discern a general human quality, the presence of this general human quality throughout the movement of history is a certainty. It cannot be expressed or defined as an abstract essence. It can only emerge in its particular forms, lurking in the most perfect works of each particular period; or, it can be seen as *"a dialectical process in history"* (my italics).

To trace the dialectical evolution of a general human quality through history would hardly qualify as an "extreme relativism"; it would, however, qualify as humanism. But even so, a relativistic procedure would entail the studying of a particular period to discover which works were considered most perfect according to the historically determined evaluation standards of the age. Then one would analyze those works to discover how the general human quality was conceived in that age. The charting of each of the period's human qualities would provide a picture of the movement through history.

But Auerbach did not proceed in that manner. He evaluated works in their various periods by the degree to which they contained a general human quality, regardless of their relative estimation within their own periods. He was not content to simply gather each period's attitudes about the general human quality; that would not do because "it is patently impossible to establish a synthesis by assembling all the particulars."[7] To the extent to which Auerbach utilized a broad and non-perspectivistic sense of a general human quality to determine which historical works were most perfect, we can consider his procedure humanistic. Auerbach's acceptance of Vico's "equation of the historical with the human" meant to him that a historical relativistic method could be incorporated to support a humanistic purpose.

Since the collection of all the relativistic particulars is insufficient to establish a synthesis, what else is required to do so? "The investigation of historical processes in the broadest sense . . . still depends very largely on the investigator's judgment, that is, on his faculty for 'rediscovering' them in his own mind. Historical research, indeed, has an exact side . . . . But where selection, interpretation (in the higher, more general sense), and classification enter into the picture, the historian's activity is far more comparable to an art than to a modern science. It is an art that works with scholarly material."[8] Thus, the art of the writer is required in order to convert the particular facts into larger patterns; and this art is not exact—not scientific or scholarly—but creative and, finally, personal.

Auerbach would have certainly agreed that when his artistic interpretation was combined with his exact, scholarly data, the result was valid and correct; but I am not sure he would have been eager to categorize his assessment as relative to his own period and milieu. He was concerned about the European crisis; beyond that (as we shall see) he was filled with portents of impending doom, of historical urgency. When the fates of lives and civilizations were at stake, his relativistic affinities became not merely superficial, but facile and irrelevant. It was then his humanistic instincts emerged; and although they were abstract, absolute, and essential, these qualities were not then so important.

Thematic presences in Erich Auerbach's writing are: an advocation of extreme historical relativism with an underlying current of humanism; a sense of historical urgency—of imminent, impending doom; and occasional moments of mystical intensity, with a yearning for transcendent peace, order, and stasis. But how did Auerbach emerge with these larger themes out of the specialized scholarly particulars he was investigating? Why did he see fit to attempt to embrace and consolidate ideas that are possibly contradictory? "My own experience, and by that I mean not merely my scientific experience, is responsible for the choice of problems, the starting points, the reasoning and the intention expressed in my writings." At the point where radical relativism is reduced to the reliability of the subjective perceptions of one man's consciousness, and where populistic humanism is conceived on that one person's consciousness as an exemplar of mankind's humanity stood Erich Auerbach: scholar, philologist, historian, creative writer. "The simple fact that a man's work stems from his existence and that consequently everything we can find out about his life serves to interpret the work loses none of its relevance because inexperienced scholars have drawn ridiculous inferences from it."[9]

For the answers to these questions, we should follow Auerbach's advice and attempt to return his work to the context of its inception, considering it not from his own relative historicistic viewpoint, but from the larger, more resonant sociological outlook that perhaps his work has helped make possible. What is significant are not merely the circumstances of Auerbach's life, but the historical events that molded and influenced him, inspiring him to ultimately adopt a stance of fervent confrontation and spirited ideological battle. Like the novelist Stendhal—one of the heroes of Auerbach's *Mimesis*—with whom he felt an emotional empathy, Erich Auerbach "lived while one earthquake after another shook the foundations of society; one of the earthquakes jarred him out of the everyday course of life prescribed for men of his station, flung him, like many of his contemporaries, into previously inconceivable adventures, events, responsibilities, tests of himself." And like his own description of Stendhal: "Such as he was, he offered himself to the moment; circumstances seized him, tossed him about, and laid upon him a unique and unexpected destiny; they formed him so that he was compelled to come to terms with reality in a way which no one had done before him."[10]

In Auerbach's case, this coming to terms with reality was simultaneously an attempt to conceive reality and to preserve and affirm it against its annihilation. When viewed in the expansive manner he had suggested, Erich Auerbach's works comprise a remarkable and heroic attempt to "impose an order upon" his life, his culture, his society, his reality:[11] for he felt, no doubt, that his entire endeavor would most probably be futile, but he knew that without his attempt there would be absolutely no hope.

Erich Auerbach was born in Berlin on November 9, 1892. He received his preliminary education at "Berlin's venerable Französisches Gymnasium, famous for its efforts to reconcile Prussian stringency with cosmopolitanism and with a strong dosage of Latin and French culture."[12] He enrolled at Heidelberg University and received his Doctor of Laws degree in 1913. His doctoral dissertation in law was concerned with the preparatory work required to institute a new penal code in Germany.[13] During the First World War he was in the German army. Upon his return from military service he decided not to pursue a career in law, but to begin work anew in order to obtain a doctorate in Romance philology at the University of Greifswald. He received his Ph.D. in 1921, with a dissertation on technique in early Renaissance novelle.[14]

It should be evident that the change in disciplines was profound: essentially, it was a movement from a profession that would function integrally within the social structure (and a dissertation that advocated change from within the social system) to a profession that would maintain a relative detachment from the society, opting to focus on esoteric problems with no apparent application to the social framework. That this change in outlook and temperament should occur for Auerbach during the First World War only solidifies our interpretation of the change. Quite possibly the violence and horrors

20

of the war contributed to the disillusionment and cynicism that would motivate a person to alter the order of his life. Whether or not distrust of system was a factor in his decision, Auerbach chose to abandon the vast, stolid legal institutions of society in order to investigate the distant shifting patterns of philological studies.

In 1923, Auerbach accepted a position as a librarian on the staff of the Prussian State Library in Berlin. Auerbach, at that time, was a man of thirty-one. Although the employment lacked the prestige and personal freedom of a university appointment, it enabled him to remain within a scholarly environment and to continue his studies, which included by now not only advanced investigations of philological problems, but an attempt to reconceive and utilize his background orientation in Hegel and German Romanticism within a literary milieu.[15] He was also actively involved in the historical speculations of Giambattista Vico, and for one who had recently decided to leave the law (with its implied continuities to the evolution of Western civilization) for Romance philology (with its textual analysis of specialized milieus), he was enthusiastic about Vico's distinction between philology (the relative truth at each particular cultural phase) and philosophy (the absolute and unchanging truth).[16] Auerbach's translation of Vico's *Scienza nuova* was published in 1924.[17]

What was primarily occupying his intellectual attention, however, was Dante's *The Divine Comedy* and its relationship to the characteristic adherence in the Ancient World to three stylistic levels: the sublime, or lofty; the intermediate; and the low, or lowly. Auerbach was fascinated by how elaborately and conclusively the ancient writers set about to categorize their world: stipulating which classes of society, and which possibilities of speech, language, storytelling, plots, and modes of presentation were appropriate to each level. He felt that their world was, as a result, static, hierarchical, hopelessly and affectedly stylized and precise, lacking vital movement and depth. He was certain that Dante's intention was to write in a sublime, or elevated, style, based on the ancient poets.

But Dante wrote the *Comedy* in the Italian vernacular; that is, he consciously utilized what had been considered in antiquity the vehicle for lowly subjects as his means to create a lofty and great artistic work. Moreover, he did not adhere to the rigid ancient categorization of subject matter; instead, he depicted a vast and varied collection of subjects, characters, and gradations between the elevated and the vulgar. Auerbach felt that this vast diversity of human possibilities was representative of life as it actually was. It was "a literary work which imitates reality and in which all imaginable spheres of reality appear: past and present, sublime grandeur and vile vulgarity, history and legend, tragic and comic occurrences, man and nature; finally, it is the story of Dante's—i.e., one single individual's—life and salvation, and thus a figure of the story of mankind's salvation in general."[18] The *Comedy* had managed to reject the ancient orders of life and, simultaneously, achieve artistic unity and a new stylistic grandeur.

But Auerbach wished to understand the essence of the *Comedy*. How could such a convincing sense of reality, with all its flux, movement, and permutation, be instilled in a work dealing with souls in the hereafter, living a "changeless existence"? The phrase "changeless existence" was originally coined by Hegel. Inspired by Hegel's comments on Dante in his Lecture on Aesthetics, Auerbach set out to investigate the intricate manifestations of realism in the *Comedy*. His particular textual observations were assembled into the construct of a dialectic: contrasting Dante's divine, eternal ahistorical goal of redemption and his character's changeless existence within the three spiritual realms, with the prevailing earthly-historical realistic quality of their expressions, descriptions, and desires. The resulting work was *Dante als Dichter der irdischen Welt*, published in 1929.[19]

Utilizing his modified Hegelian analysis, Auerbach asserted the primacy of a historical, earthly existence within the eternal plan: for it was one's brief life that determined the assessment of God and one's eternal fate in the hereafter. It was all a prolonged attempt at expanding the realms of Vico's theory of historical knowledge. Vico had asserted that the world of nature was created by God, according to His plan; but since the history of man, or the world of nations, was created by man, that much could be understood by him. Now Auerbach was proposing (as manifest in the *Comedy*) that since man's history was responsible for determining his eternal life, the earthly sphere of man's history could exert some role in determining the nature of God's world.

At any rate, on the basis of this volume, Erich Auerbach was appointed to the chair of Romance philology at the University of Marburg in 1929. He was then thirty-seven years old. To be initiating one's first professional appointment at a relatively advanced age required a considerable degree of patience, ambition, and personal vision. For indeed, had not the First World War occurred, impelling him to reorder his priorities, he might by then have been a prosperous attorney or professor of law; or else, had he decided to switch to philology in any case, without the war he might have had the opportunity to produce more prolifically, thus facilitating earlier recognition in his field. It is not difficult to appreciate how an argument that man's choices and his historical existence affect his ultimate eternal destiny had a particular appeal to Auerbach.

At the same time, however, he was troubled by the description of Dante that was presented in his book. Certainly, the study was inconclusive: he lacked a conceptualization that was distinctive, discrete from Hegelian influences, and representative of his own philosophical intuitions with which to support his particular explications; he had not obtained a philological explanation for the phenomena in the *Comedy* he had already isolated. He was "concerned with the question what conception of the structure of events, in other words what conception of history, is the foundation for Dante's realism, this realism projected into changeless eternity." He wanted to explore more extensively "Dante's elevated style, for [it] consists precisely in integrating what is characteristically individual and at times horrible, ugly, grotesque, and vulgar with the dignity of

God's judgment—a dignity which transcends the ultimate limits of our earthly conception of the sublime."[20]

At the time of his university appointment in 1929, Auerbach had lived much of his life in Berlin. It is interesting to consider Auerbach's emerging philological concerns from within the context of the larger artistic movement in Berlin during the twenties. To cite one example: in 1924 an art gallery director in Berlin, Dr. Gustav Hartlaub, opened an exhibition called "The New Objectivity." He noted the "inclination of many artists toward a more literal representation of their physical surroundings." There was, he wrote, a "general contemporary feeling in Germany of resignation and cynicism after a period of exuberant hopes . . . . the positive side expresses itself in the enthusiasm for the immediate reality . . . the desire to take things entirely objectively . . . without immediately investing them with ideal implications."[21]

One of the artists in Hartlaub's show was George Grosz, who was motivated after his military service in the First World War to depict in his drawings the grotesque, the bizarre, the horrendous, and scenes of squalid low life.[22] In addition, Hartlaub suggested, in the same passage, that the new architecture of such men as Walter Gropius should also be considered representative of the New Objectivity. Finally, the plays of Bertolt Brecht—with their consideration of the plight of the proletariat, and his new ideas about the audience's participation in a dramatic work—were becoming popular in the city.

These artistic concepts were evident in Auerbach's work by that time. His concern for what was sublime, intermediate, and lowly led him to examine those elements of the *Comedy* that were "horrible, ugly, grotesque, and vulgar," those elements that embodied the temporal and worldly. He referred to them as low subjects, or styles, and began to think of the lowly as being in dialectical opposition to the sublime. Auerbach classified Dante's depiction of these elements as imitation of reality and realistic; he was starting to associate the lowly with the realistic, equating them with the notion of a basic human quality.

At the University of Marburg, Auerbach must have savored his new position with its accompanying prestige, the challenge and gratification of teaching classes, and the relative time and opportunity (when compared to the hours of a professional librarian) that he could now devote to his scholarly pursuits. But in late 1932 Adolf Hitler was elected Chancellor of Germany, and by March of 1933 he had consolidated his power to dictatorial proportion. As a Jew, Erich Auerbach had cause to be concerned about the new racial policies, and with the series of edicts and regulations that proceeded to categorize German society according to the racial discrimination of that time.

In April 1933 the law distinguishing "non-Aryans" from the general population was proclaimed and enforced. By 1935, Erich Auerbach was forced to leave his position at the University of Marburg; in total, he had been employed as a professor for six years, and the last two, imbued as they were with an oppressive atmosphere of resentment and brutality, must have been difficult to endure.

In Germany at that time, there was also a pervasive campaign to redefine and revise the distinctive qualities of the culture in order to align them with the new racial categories and restrictions. Serious scholarship was by no means exempt from national scrutiny, especially scholarly investigations of Christianity and the early Middle Ages. A virulent controversy was raging: since Christianity regarded as sacred the Old Testament, since the Old Testament was the Jewish Bible, since Christ had lived his life as a Jew, how could Christianity—with its "non-Aryan" roots—be compatible with the goals and heritage of National Socialism?

That dubious intellectual climate prevailed during the final years of Auerbach's appointment at Marburg. The climate, with its particular emphasis and argument, was to exert an influence on the major work of Auerbach as soon as he left Germany. A selection from

Erich Auerbach

what was a moderate view at the time will serve to illustrate the spirit
of the times. These remarks are excerpted from a sermon delivered by
Cardinal Faulhaber in Munich in 1933:

*Already in the year 1899, and on the occasion of an anti-Semitic demon-
stration at Hamburg . . . a demand was raised for the total separation of
Judaism from Christianity, and for the complete elimination from Christianity of all Jewish elements. . . . Today these single voices have swelled
together into a chorus: Away with the Old Testament! A Christianity
which still clings to the Old Testament is a Jewish religion, irreconcilable
with the spirit of the German people. . . .*

*Even the Person of Christ is not spared by this religious revolution.
Some have indeed tried to save Him with a forged birth certificate and have
said that He was not a Jew at all but an Aryan. . . . But so long as
historical sources count for more than surmise, there can be no doubt about
the fact. . . . He was entered in the register as a descendent of David. And
so others now take up the cry: Then we must renounce Him, if He was a
Jew. . . .*

*When racial research, in itself not a religious matter, makes war upon
religion and attacks the foundations of Christianity; when antagonism to
the Jews of the present day is extended to the sacred books of the Old
Testament and Christianity is condemned because it has relations of origin
with pre-Christian Judaism . . . then the bishop cannot remain silent. . . .*

*So that I may be perfectly clear . . . let me begin by making three
distinctions. We must first distinguish between the people of Israel before
and after the death of Christ. Before the death of Christ during the period
between the calling of Abraham and the fullness of time, the people of
Israel were the vehicle of Divine Revelation. . . .*

*After the death of Christ, Israel was dismissed from the service of
Revelation. She had not known the time of her visitation. She had re-
pudiated and rejected the Lord's Anointed, had driven Him out of the city
and nailed Him to the Cross. Then the veil of the Temple was rent, and
with it the covenant between the Lord and His people. . . .*

. . . We must distinguish between the Scriptures of the Old Testament

on the one hand and the Talmudic writings of post-Christian Judaism on the other. . . . We must distinguish in the Old Testament Bible itself between what had only transitory value and what had permanent value. The long genealogies had value in ancient times, but their value was not permanent; similarly, the numerous regulations for the ancient sacrifices and ceremonial cleansings.

. . . We do not set the Old Testament and the New on the same level. The Sacred Scriptures of the New Testament . . . must hold the place of honor. . . . By accepting these books Christianity does not become a Jewish religion. These books were not composed by Jews; they are inspired by the Holy Ghost . . . they are the word of God. . . . Antagonism to the Jews of today must not be extended to the books of pre-Christian Judaism. . . .

From the Church's point of view there is no objection whatever to racial research and race culture. Nor is there any objection to the endeavor to keep the national characteristics of a people as far as possible pure and unadulterated, and to foster their national spirit by emphasis upon the common ties which unite them. . . .

What is the relation of Christianity to the German race? Race and Christianity are not mutually opposed, but they do belong to different orders. Race is of the natural order; Christianity is a revealed religion and therefore of the supernatural order. Race means union with the nation; Christianity means primarily union with God. . . .

The Christian, so long as he observes the above conditions, is not forbidden to stand up for his race and his rights. It is possible, therefore, without divided allegiance, to be an upright German and at the same time an upright Christian. [23]

Several aspects of this argument were directly applicable to Auerbach and his study of the realism in the *Comedy*. The central underlying principle of the sermon was the distinction between the natural order and the order of salvation; the political state held jurisdiction in the first, but the second was the realm of the Church. That argument had been used during the Middle Ages, and Auerbach was keenly aware of its past and the contemporary variations on it. Cardinal Faulhaber emphasized the following: there is a distinction between Jews before and after the death of Christ; the Old Testament was not composed by Jews, but by the word of God; the historical post–Old Testament books of the Jews—such as the Talmud—are not sacred; modern Jews are severed from Revelation; the ceremonial laws and the historical genealogies of the Old Testament are no longer valid; one can observe the principles of National Socialism, provided that one honors the rights and provinces of the Church.

Without any means of employment in Germany, Auerbach accepted an appointment as professor of Romance languages at the Istanbul State University in Turkey. The opportunity to resume scholarly pursuits was enthusiastically embraced by many German intellectual émigrés at the time. The situation, though, was not without its difficulties. When compared to the rigorous and sophisticated academic atmosphere and facilities in Germany, the level of scholarship and the materials for research were woefully inadequate.[24] Auerbach had arrived in Istanbul with the notes, references, and citations for his work in progress; but he realized that after completing those articles he would no longer be able to continue the type of in-depth scholarly investigations into ancient and medieval philological problems to which he had become accustomed. Yet the position in Istanbul allowed him the relative safety and means to continue to write; and, from Istanbul, he could view with detachment and perspective not only the significance of the contemporary events in Germany and Europe, but the entire evolution of literature in Western Europe.

Before he could come to terms with his new and trying working conditions, Auerbach had still to complete the work he had been engaged in before he fled Germany. There were two significant concerns in his mind: one was to discover the ultimate underlying basis for the realistic tendencies he had observed in Dante; the other was the critical political situation in Europe, which had produced tracts similar to Cardinal Faulhaber's (and others far less moderate). Those tracts had been responsible for his expulsion from Germany, and their violent conflict of ideologies would soon engulf the continent.

Auerbach believed that the historical actuality of National Socialism was integrally related to the attitudes that the political, social, and religious institutions of the time adopted toward it. The position advocated by the Church in Germany that contributed to the continuing existence of the government was similar to the Church's position during the Middle Ages. He saw that the contemporary manifestation of history was such that by writing one philological article, he could simultaneously explain a remote stylistic tendency and assert his topical protest against the spread of totalitarianism. But that was not all. Auerbach began to see that if his analysis of the evolution of Western literature was correct—that is, if there was indeed a historical connection between the human realistic element in the greatest works of our culture—then to affirm and explain the realistic essence of Dante was the equivalent of bolstering and defending the humanity of his own civilization.

The result was "Figura," one of Erich Auerbach's most important works.[25] In it he refers to his own earlier study of Dante and the dominance of the earthly sphere in a work and world devoted to the spiritual: "At that time I lacked a solid historical grounding for this view, which is already to be found in Hegel and which is the basis of my interpretation of the *Divine Comedy*; it is suggested rather than formulated in the introductory chapters of the book. I believe that I have now found this historical grounding; it is precisely the figural interpretation of reality which, though in constant conflict with purely spiritualist and Neoplatonic tendencies, was the dominant view in the European Middle Ages."[26]

To arrive at this concept of figural interpretation, Auerbach presents a learned and impressive etymology of the word *figura* from its earliest manifestations in Latin antiquity, through the original phenomenal prophecy of the church fathers, up to and including the medieval utilization in Dante's *Divine Comedy*, "the work which concludes and sums up the culture of the Middle Ages." On the basis

Erich Auerbach

of his scholarly evidence he concludes that *"figura* is something real and historical." He emphasizes that "real historical figures are to be interpreted spiritually. . . . but the interpretation points to a carnal, hence historical fulfillment . . . for the truth has become history or flesh" (Auerbach, "Figura," in *Scenes*, pp. 64, 29, 34).

Here is how Auerbach explains figural interpretation:

Figural interpretation establishes a connection between two events or persons, the first of which signifies not only itself but also the second, while the second encompasses or fulfills the first. The two poles of the figure are separate in time, but both, being real events or figures, are within time, within the stream of historical life. Only the understanding of the two persons or events is a spiritual act, but this spiritual act deals with concrete events whether past, present, or future, and not with concepts or abstractions; these are quite secondary, since promise and fulfillment are real historical events, which have either happened in the incarnation of the Word, or will happen in the second coming.[Auerbach, "Figura," in *Scenes*, p. 53]

According to Auerbach, figural interpretation is not merely a conception by which an event in the Old Testament was said to prophesy the occurrence of an event in the New Testament (Auerbach refers to the event that predicts as "figure," and the subsequent event that was predicted and occurs as "fulfillment"), but an interpretation of history and the principal events that shaped the culture and civilization of Western Europe.

Thus, the emerging Christian religion was able to transform "the Old Testament from a book of laws and a history of the people of Israel into a series of figures of Christ and the Redemption, such as we find later in the procession of prophets in the medieval theatre and in the cyclic representations of medieval sculpture" (Auerbach, "Figura" in *Scenes*, p. 52). This transformation of the Old Testament into a prophetic work aided in the acceptance of Christianity, for it added to the religion a broad sweep of historical inevitability and supernatural determinism, without which it would have been unlikely for the outlying cultures (Auerbach cites the Celtic and Germanic peoples) to adopt it as their own.

The essential notion, however, is that figural interpretation not only transformed the nature of the Old Testament, but *preserved and affirmed its historical essence*: "But actually there is no choice between historical and hidden meaning; both are present. The figural structure preserves the historical event while interpreting it as revelation; and must preserve it in order to interpret it" (Auerbach, "Figura," in *Scenes*, p. 68). Each person and event is not only related to every other by the horizontal procession of history; also, and simultaneously, every person and event is encompassed by, and individually and particularly related (Auerbach terms this vertical relation) to the ultimate person (Christ) and the ultimate event (His Resurrection). In this notion we can designate the basis of a concept of realism that Auerbach linked to the figural method of interpretation, and that he asserted became the framework of Western literature: a realism that would be concerned with the lowly manifestations of history, elaborately depicting their historical essence (or low qualities) and yet, conceiving each as connected with the Ultimate and, therefore, sublime, significant, and worthy of serious treatment and tone.[27]

As Auerbach applied the laws of figural interpretation, we are able to grasp the profound interpretative changes that ensue in the history of our culture. He writes:

It was not until very late, probably not until after the Reformation, that Europeans began to regard the Old Testament as Jewish history and Jewish law; it first came to the newly converted peoples as figura rerum *or phenomenal prophecy, as a prefiguration of Christ, so giving them a basic conception of history, which derived its compelling force from its inseparable bond with the faith, and which for almost a thousand years remained the only accepted view of history. Consequently the attitude embodied in the figural interpretation became one of the essential elements of the Christian picture of reality, history, and the concrete world in general.*[28]

Auerbach is really asserting that the arguments of Cardinal Faulhaber and others—that there was a distinction between Jews before and after the death of Christ—were invalid; for even when the Europeans were originally adopting the Old Testament as a book of figures for the New Testament, they were, by the very essence of the figural process, embracing and adopting the history and laws of the Jewish people. And it was this figural interpretation that influenced for a thousand years our European notions of history, culture, religion, and reality.

Thus, it was impossible to venerate the religious laws of pre-Christian Jews (at that time they were "the vehicle of Divine Revelation"), and to abhor them afterward (and at the present) since they were dismissed from the service of God. To incorporate the early history of the Jews as the word of God predicting the coming of Christ was also to incorporate their historical essence—the laws, beliefs, and corporality of their lives. Hence, there was only one choice (or, as Auerbach arranged it, no choice): one could embrace one's Christianity (and with it, one's Christian and, therefore, Western culture, civilization, reality) in all its ultimate grandeur and sublimity, but one had to realize that in order for it to be prefigured in history and ultimate, one had to embrace the same historical existence and laws and customs of the Jewish people—from which Christianity is inseparable (and these laws and customs are the qualities of contemporary Jews in Germany), or else one could persecute the Jews, embrace "Germany" (a spurious term, for it could not have existed without its Christian heritage) and National Socialism, and therefore deny all one's traditions, cultural products, and benefits of civilization—in effect, return to the relative barbarity of pre-Christian Germanic tribes. Because of the very process by which Christianity had become Christianity the religion, the culture was intrinsically Judeo-Christian; to denigrate that fact was to deny oneself.

Auerbach went further than that. He returned to the writings of the early church fathers in order to demonstrate that they, in their use of figural interpretation, were incorporating the Old Testament as both historical and figural, and that the process was ongoing, for ultimate fulfillment was still in the future:

> But the "heavenly" fulfillment is not complete, and consequently, as in certain earlier writers but more definitely in Augustine, the confrontation of the two poles, figure and fulfillment, is sometimes replaced by a development in three stages: the Law or history of the Jews as a prophetic figura *for the appearance of Christ; the incarnation as fulfillment of this* figura *and at the same time as a new promise of the end of the world and the Last Judgement; and finally, the future occurrence of these events as ultimate fulfillment.* [29]

Through his painstakingly precise tracing of the forms of the word *figura*, Auerbach was able to make his point abundantly clear: prefiguration was inseparable from historical existence; so in order for the Last Judgment to be prefigured by the incarnation, Christ must be prefigured by the Law and history of the Jews. It is impossible to claim (as did the cardinal) that one of the parts had become outmoded; each event or person was functionally linked by the ongoing flow of history and by the single event that incorporates them all and transcends history—the life of Christ. To further emphasize that his conception is applicable to contemporary political reality as well as to medieval philology, Auerbach points out parallels between the medieval Church policies and those that were being debated in Germany in his comment on Augustine's conception of "the latter-day Jews, and here [Augustine] strikes a theme which was to run through all subsequent polemics against the Jews, refused in their obdurate blindness to recognize [the incarnation]" (Auerbach, "Figura," in *Scenes*, p. 40).

The article remains, however, a studious etymology of the word and its applications in medieval literature, culminating in Dante. (But it is one characteristic of Auerbach's development in response to the events of his day that as he tends to become increasingly suspicious of generalities and ideologies—identifying them with totalitarian

33

systems—he invests the particular with a resonance and applicability that is ultimately rooted in the personal: a mystical assertion that one man's extreme relative concerns can close the gap and connect.) And here Auerbach demonstrates that Dante possessed a conception of history that was shaped by figural interpretation. For instance, he utilized characters from antiquity in symbolic postures with implications that were problematic to Christian doctrine. But Auerbach demonstrates that Dante was not utilizing allegory or mythical structures but figural interpretation. So the characters from ancient Rome were not only historical actors, but figures of the appearance of Christ. Auerbach thus clarifies Dante's use of Virgil as his guide and model, and Dante's purpose in presenting Cato of Utica. "For Dante the meaning of every life has its place in the providential history of the world, the general lines of which are laid down in the Revelation which has been given to every Christian" (Auerbach, "Figura," in *Scenes*, pp. 70–71).

The isolation and description of a method of conceiving history proved fruitful to Auerbach not merely as the framework upon which he wanted to hang his observations about realism in the *Comedy*. He had delineated a mode of interpretation in which lowly historical figures and events were able to remain historical, yet were invested with an exalted stature as a result of their connection with an all-encompassing grandiose conception. Both figure and fulfillment were historically related—in a lowly manner—through their appearances in the evolution of history. Both were also supernaturally related—in a sublime manner—through their relative participation in the story of Christ.

In his remarkable "Figura" essay, he uses his discovery to explicate literary materials, but he develops its possibilities in such a way that the application of figural interpretation assaults the principles of National Socialism and the notions of racial purity. We can observe the increasing awareness in Auerbach of the larger ramifications of figural interpretation in passages such as this:

Thus the figures are not only tentative; they are also the tentative form of

something eternal and timeless; they point not only to the concrete future,
but also to something that always has been and always will be; they point
to something which is in need of interpretation, which will indeed be
fulfilled in the concrete future, but which is at all times present, fulfilled in
God's providence, which knows no difference of time. This eternal thing is
already figured in them, and thus they are both tentative fragmentary
reality, and veiled eternal reality.[30]

Figural interpretation had already asserted that Jewish laws, customs, derivations, and philosophies were an intrinsic—and inseparable—part of Western culture.

But as his article appeared, the conflict that had existed within
Germany began to spread throughout Europe and threaten the Western world. The lines of confrontation were apparent; what emerges in
the above passage is Auerbach's increasing sense that what was
required was a militant interpretation of the civilization under attack,
an interpretation that would affirm, validate, and revitalize the very
qualities of that civilization that nazism and fascism were determined to destroy.

Bolstering Auerbach's sense of his historical function in the world
conflict was his professional situation in Istanbul; it rapidly became
evident through several incidents (undoubtedly, both comic and
frustrating for Auerbach) that his contribution to the Istanbul State
University would remain on a level that was, at once, basic, elementary, superficial, and wasteful. For instance, Auerbach was introduced to the Turkish translator of the *Divine Comedy* who, although
he knew no Italian, had worked from a French translation (which he
subsequently lost), and had completed his task in less than two
years.[31] Auerbach also found it useful to write a basic handbook on
Romance languages and literature, so that his Turkish students
would have at least an elementary grasp of his lectures and concerns.[32] It contained introductory sections on philology, Western
literary history, and Christianity. And during most of his residence
in Istanbul, Auerbach had no access to the journals, volumes, or other
publications of Western Europe.

With the publication of "Figura" and a few other related articles on Dante, Erich Auerbach had exhausted the scholarly materials that he had brought with him to Istanbul. He was then in his late forties and in an awkward position. The entire movement of his career thus far had dictated that one's efforts and trust should be devoted to the particular, the specific, but the limited library facilities precluded highly detailed philological work. Any project he undertook would have to substitute breadth of vision for in-depth examination.

But as the world situation deteriorated, Auerbach found himself increasingly concerned; with this concern was the realization that he was detached from the conflict. Although the world crisis was urgent and critical, he was in a society that was outside the central scope of the conflicting cultures and ideologies. He was not only able to view the conflict from a larger perspective than before, he was also able to conceive and interpret the significance of the literary history and cultural development that led up to the crisis. The historical situation had placed him in a position with a unique vantage point. It was up to him to rise to the opportunity. Could he afford to indulge in minutiae, waiting for the conflict to subside? Hardly, for the fate of his world hung in the balance. Romance philology would not exist if the wrong side were to win. So Erich Auerbach, radical relativist, began to work on a broad-based study that would examine the depiction of reality from ancient times to the present.

He brought with him to the task the concepts he had previously developed from his philological research. He knew that an outstanding characteristic of antiquity was the categorization of style and subject, and he had already begun to oppose the lowly with the sublime. Dante had broken out of this mode and initiated a new mixed style, one that contained a realism which was filled with the general quality of life because the roots of its conception were in the figural interpretation. And this figural approach centered on the story of Christ: for when Christ appeared in human form and lived among the lowly people he was not only descending from the sublime to the low, he was transcending those categories, enabling the lowly citizens to be filled with grandeur through him. Auerbach, however, saw that the effect of figural interpretation diminished as the years passed and the Last Judgment was no longer imminent.

In Istanbul, he saw that a philosophy of realism could utilize the principles of figural interpretation and revise them to a post-Christian, that is, historically relative, society. The same unity of the historically lowly with the Absolute sublime would serve to treat people of lower historical and economic class and level with unprecedented seriousness and importance. Thus, realism would be infused with the general human quality; and that human quality would transcend and encompass the historically particular. And like the Christianity from which it arose, that realism would take the common man and transform his humanity into an essence both sublime and eternal.

The methodology he would employ was as much as possible a concession to his belief in the representational truth of isolated particularities: for each period of literary history, he selected a group of texts for explication. At first, the discussion was confined to the passage, but gradually the implications and realms of the problem would expand until the most significant matters were under consideration. Auerbach hoped that this method would maintain his orientation in the particular validity, but above all he wanted the reader to perceive the scope of his discussion without being distracted by irrelevant minor details: "The procedure I have employed—that of citing for every epoch a number of texts and using these as test cases for my ideas—takes the reader directly into the subject and makes him sense what is at issue long before he is expected to cope with anything theoretical."[33]

Auerbach worked on the book from May 1942 through April 1945 but, in a very real sense, it utilized and incorporated all the philological work he had ever done, all of his studies in law, history, philosophy. The completed work—*Mimesis. Dargestellte Wirklichkeit in der abendländischen Literatur*—was published in Bern in 1946; it was acclaimed by a majority of critics as one of the most essential works of literary criticism of the century. We shall see, however, that for the most part the book was not received as Auerbach had meant it.

The dates of composition appear in the book: Auerbach's way of emphasizing that *Mimesis* was a product of a specific historical period and should be understood in relation to that period. The inscription, taken from Andrew Marvell's "To His Coy Mistress"—"Had we but world enough and time . . ."—would seem, were this a standard book of literary history, to be a modest and whimsical assessment of the author's aims in relation to his finished product. Considering what we know about Auerbach's intellectual development up to this point, it is clear that the quotation is designed to reflect the urgency, the desperation, and the gravity from which Auerbach conceived it.

The first section of the book compares and sets into opposition two exemplary literary styles: those of Homer and the Old Testament. He compares the scene of Odysseus' homecoming (when he is recognized by his old housekeeper because of a familiar scar on his leg) with the scene of God's appearance to Abraham (when Abraham was commanded to sacrifice his son, Isaac). Auerbach points out that at the moment of tension, when the housekeeper recognizes the scar, Homer pauses to present an elaborate account of how young Odysseus received the scar as a boy on a hunt. This digression is presented by Homer as if it were equal in importance to the tense recognition scene. Auerbach terms it "uniform illumination" and summarizes that: "the basic impulse of the Homeric style: [is] to represent phenomena in a fully externalized form, visible and palpable in all their parts, and completely fixed in their spatial and temporal relations" (Auerbach, *Mimesis*, p. 6). Homer, according to Auerbach, has no interest in the inner psychology of his characters, and the extended narrative of the childhood accident is not included to increase the suspense. Indeed, "the Homeric poems . . . prevent the reader from concentrating exclusively on a present crisis; even when the most terrible things are occurring, they prevent the establishment of an overwhelming suspense" (Auerbach, *Mimesis*, p. 11).

The scene from the Bible is narrated with only selective details:

those that are included are often symbolic and ambiguous. The effect is not, as in Homer, to emphasize the external detail, but to "indicate thoughts which remain unexpressed." In the biblical style there is:

the externalization of only so much of the phenomena as is necessary for the purpose of the narrative, all else is left in obscurity . . . time and place are undefined and call for interpretation; thoughts and feeling remain unexpressed, are only suggested by the silence and the fragmentary speeches; the whole, permeated with the most unrelieved suspense and directed toward a single goal. [Auerbach, *Mimesis*, pp. 11–12]

Although Auerbach praises the brilliance of Homer's depiction, he is clearly more excited, more interested by the elements in the Old Testament; he declares that emotions and situations of such profundity, psychological complexity, and emotional power (as in the Bible) would be beyond the scope of Homer's characters, "whose destiny is clearly defined and who wake up every morning as if it were the first day of their lives" (Auerbach, *Mimesis*, p. 12). The good-natured sarcasm here is perceived at first to be a consequence of the apt literary and philological observation. Actually, Auerbach is subtly constructing his lines of conflict, and his objectivity is merely a pose.

Auerbach explains that the Homeric style reflects the qualities of the society it describes, but Auerbach's designation of that society is in a language far removed from his earlier philological observations "in the Homeric poems life is enacted only among the ruling class . . . a sort of feudal aristocracy, whose men divide their lives between war, hunting, marketplace councils, and feasting, while the women supervise the maids in the house. As a social picture, this world is completely stable" (Auerbach, *Mimesis*, p. 21). In contrast, the society of the Bible is "much less stable; class distinctions are not felt"; the "people [possess] the irrepressible politico-religious spontaneity." He goes on to describe Homer as legend, and the Bible as written history, or at least, material that makes absolute claim to being history. Legend, by his definition, simplifies and stylizes its material, thus separating it from the particular historical context to which it belongs. In contrast to the straightforward and clarified depiction of legend, historical accounts are ambiguous, uncertain, filled with contradiction; they are also profound, evocative, and meaningful. They insist on interpretation and enlargement. And as subjective representations of the particular historical period, they are closer to the general human quality that runs through time. Legend seeks to provide entertainment; history aims for meaning, truth. From Auerbach's vantage point, one is clearly preferable to the other: "Far from seeking, like Homer, merely to make us forget our own reality for a few hours, [the Bible] seeks to overcome our reality: we are to fit our own life into its world, feel ourselves to be elements in its structure of universal history" (Auerbach, *Mimesis*, pp. 21, 60).

Even as Auerbach formulates his advocacy of a historical realistic style, his belief in the validity of the personal or subjective perspective leads him to an interesting formulation, one that embraces the existential verity of the personal consciousness caught up in the dramatic movement of history:

The reader clearly feels how the extent of the pendulum's swing is connected with the intensity of the personal history—precisely the most extreme circumstances, in which we are immeasurably forsaken and in despair, or immeasurably joyous and exalted, give us, if we survive them, a personal stamp which is recognized as the product of a rich existence, a rich development. [34]

Here we can see the beginnings of Auerbach's attempt to expand the context of his figural interpretation system: the humanistic flow of history, when it descends to incorporate the life of a particular man, elicits from him the general human quality that transcends all periods and is present—in fluidity—throughout time (the history is substituted for the role of Christ; the continuity of man's human quality through time is substituted for eternal life). Auerbach begins to assert its existence now, so that its presence will be synonymous with Western civilization but predate the origins of Christianity. In the modern crisis, then, when the revolutionary power of Christ has deteriorated through the Church's long coexistence with the corrupting state, the power of history's humanity will yet prevail against the barbarism of totalitarianism. And lest we fail to see the modern context that delineates the predicament, Auerbach calls attention—in the very first chapter—to the rise of nazism in Germany, and to the Second World War and how tempting it is, when caught in the Nazi grasp, to lapse into legend in order to simplify and nullify the experience.

In the earliest phase of his investigation of realistic representation in Western literature, Auerbach has masterfully described the distinctive qualities of the two most important early styles. On another level, however, he has invested the Homeric style and reality with certain nonliterary characteristics: static, hierarchical, rigidly consigning its reality into frozen categories and classifying labels, superficial, and elitist. Similarly, he has attributed to the Old Testament style and reality the following: a movement of events, personalities, and social classes; a profound conception of life and existence; and the basis for a demotic human movement founded on the equality of all men. Further, he begins to indicate his affinity with the representational realism of the Old Testament.

In the second section of *Mimesis*, Auerbach begins with the feast of Trimalchio from Petronius's *Satyricon*. In describing this scene, Auerbach proceeds in an unexpected manner when considered according to our interpretation of his intent: he contrasts Petronius with Homer and concludes that Petronius is far more realistic. This would appear to be odd—not the observation, for indeed, the literary mimetic quality is far greater in Petronius—for we would think Auerbach would wish to demonstrate the rigid limitations of ancient texts and their methods of viewing life, in opposition to the life-affirming possibilities of the biblical, and Western, view. Thus, we are not surprised when Auerbach grants the relative realism of Petronius, but then criticizes it for its intentions and limitations, which are at one with Homer.

"In the mimetic literary art of antiquity," writes Auerbach, "the instability of fortune almost always appears as a fate which strikes from without and affects only a limited area, not as a fate which results from the inner processes of the real, historical world" (Auerbach, *Mimesis*, p. 29). Petronius, then, is not ultimately serious about depicting a dynamic society, for his changes descend from fate, instead of emerging from the depths of humanity. Such is his sophistication that he would evoke fluidity only for the purpose of entertainment, not as a social reality. Again, one would think that as a relativist, Auerbach would assert the validity of the ancient conception of fate when viewed from its historical context. But since Auerbach is also attempting to delineate two differentiated strands of attitudes toward life and reality that culminate in his contemporary society, he cannot do this.

This description of the limitations of Homer and the ancient writers provides a clue to the way in which Auerbach was considering the qualities of ancient literature and what he associated them with in his own period: "Homer's Greek audiences are schooled in mythology and genealogy; Homer undertakes to give them the family-tree of the character in question as a means of placing him. *Just so, in modern times, a newcomer into an exclusive aristocratic or bourgeois society can be placed by information concerning his paternal and maternal relatives.* Thus, rather than an impression of historical change, Homer evokes the illusion of *an unchanging,* a basically *stable social order, in comparison with which the succession of individuals and changes in personal fortunes appear unimportant*" (Auerbach, *Mimesis*, p. 28; my italics). Much of the material that I have underscored was not necessary for the establishment of Auerbach's literary point. The additional words are included in order to establish lines of association Auerbach wishes to emphasize—a nucleus of consistent qualities and tendencies that he wants to set against the Western humanistic reality. "Just so, in modern times," he writes, in order to demonstrate that Homer's genealogy is not so very different from the Nazi "Aryanization" laws, which traced back one's ancestors to three or four removed generations.

Homer's mythology is not so different from the new mythology of the Thousand-Year Reich and its *Volkstaat*. The fates of individuals that are ignored and the changes in personal fortune carelessly induced by the elitist Greeks are related to the oppressive measures against peoples in Germany, not the least of which is causing a learned professor of Romance philology to be writing in Istanbul without books, journals, sources, or adequate library. Certainly, Auerbach is not equating these tendencies; rather, he wishes to display an evolution that will culminate in the dramatic realization of the current crisis and underline precisely which qualities have not been responsible or implicated and therefore must be preserved.

Auerbach dispenses with Petronius as a serious realist because his realism is satiric, not sincere, and he proceeds from ethical rather than from economic, political, or historical motives. When Auerbach next presents a passage from Tacitus, it would again seem that, from a relativistic context, he has found a realism that is historical and comparatively populistic from an ancient standard. Tacitus describes a spontaneous address to a group of Roman legions by a common soldier, an address devoted to detailing their grievances and complaints. Auerbach admits that this would appear to be realistic, but then explains why even this passage is not satisfactory: "For Tacitus not only lacks understanding, he actually has no interest whatever in the facts underlying the soldier's demands" (Auerbach, *Mimesis*, p. 37). Auerbach's point is that a humanistic realism cannot afford simply to depict the demands and desires of a lowly social group in a mimetic manner. Instead, it must represent the group and its demands, view them objectively, and be sincerely interested in them. If disagreement is then still possible, this must be done with reason, civility, and a sense of fair play.

It can be seen, I think, that Auerbach's analysis of the representation of reality throughout history is not primarily geared to be literary history or philology, for the kinds of judgments and distinctions he is making would not be agreeable to him were he proceeding solely along those lines (or according to his principles—discussed

43

above—of philological scholarship). Once again, Auerbach provides the association he wants to dominate the discussion and offer focus for his argument. The incident Tacitus presents, Auerbach asserts, is not a full-fledged socio-historical movement. But even if there were such a movement, Tacitus would have felt the need to present the argument and recognize it, as did conservative politicians in recent years when they responded to the questions raised by socialist politicians, even though they disagreed. What would this observation possibly have to do with Tacitus? Auerbach replies that Tacitus did not need to respond, for there were no opposing social or historical groups; nor was there a conception of social or historical factors. Why is Auerbach not content to grant the observation and accept it from a perspectivistic viewpoint? Because the ancient world

does not see forces, it sees vices and virtues, successes and mistakes. Its formulation of problems is not concerned with historical developments either intellectual or material, but with ethical judgements . . . [it is] based upon an aristocratic reluctance to become involved with growth processes in the depths, for these processes are felt to be both vulgar and orgiastically lawless. [Auerbach, *Mimesis*, p. 38]

And any modern society that likewise prohibits discussion and social fluidity, and that emphasizes ethical modes of life based on artificial and tyrannical conceptions of perfection and failure, a priori assumptions of vice and virtue, is proceeding according to the principles of antiquity, which are staid, vapid, nonhumanistic, and elitist.

In opposition to the regulation of styles in antiquity, Auerbach presents the scene of Peter's denial in the New Testament, a psychologically sensitive treatment of an essentially low figure. But the depiction of Peter, "a tragic figure from such a background, a hero of such weakness, who yet derives the highest force from his very weakness, such a to and fro of the pendulum, is incompatible with the sublime style of classical antique literature" (Auerbach, *Mimesis*, p. 42). And this is to be assumed, since "the greatest writers possess a realistic knowledge of the human heart which, though it is soberly based on experience, is never mean" (Auerbach, *Mimesis*, p. 40). What is imperative in these times for Auerbach is a sense of urgency and commitment, the willingness to assert one's fervent support for an affirmative conception of humanity and one's opposition to any tyranny that compromises mankind or its humanity. This is the current crisis. If, in the process of such a crucial defense, some notions of historical relativism and philological perspectivism are revised or reinterpreted, it is not so important; without our effort now, there may be no constructive life tomorrow. What Auerbach does not concede is that when a man is moved to such a degree of concern and principle, he has compromised radical relativism and asserted a basic and underlying morality.

Auerbach's need to dwell on what is decent, constructive, and communal among men as an answer to the formalized, ornate, and lifeless patterns of National Socialism becomes increasingly pressing as he attempts to deal with writers of the late antiquity because of the qualities he isolates in the writing, qualities that he associates with his own historical period. The writer Ammianus possessed a humor that always had "an element of bitterness, of the grotesque, very often of something grotesquely gruesome and inhumanly convulsive." Such humor was derived from the overall situation in Ammianus's world. His world, according to Auerbach, "is somber: it is full of superstition, blood frenzy, exhaustion, fear of death, and grim and magically rigid gestures." And how can the literature not reflect this sordid quality, when the people in the society "live between a frenzy of bloodshed and mortal terror"? (Auerbach, *Mimesis*, pp. 56, 55). But the notion that a deteriorating and decadent society would inspire a literature which is excessive, grotesque, and subterranean is applicable to a kind of mimetic theory; for if the qualities within the literature can be demonstrated to exist within the social and historical environment, then the literature represents the essence of the historical period and the literary history of an age would provide the crucial aspects of any larger history.

That an author's work might depict an age is an idea that would interest any literary historian attempting to outline the path of Western literature. But it was not of primary interest to Erich Auerbach. It is not sufficient for a writer to describe the social reality of his age; he must do more, and Auerbach describes this in an emotional passage that is simultaneously about Ammianus and Auerbach himself:

Ammianus' world is very often a caricature of the normal human environment in which we live; very often it is like a bad dream. This is not simply because horrible things happen in it—treason, torture, persecution, denunciations: such things are prevalent in almost all times and places, and the periods when life is somewhat more tolerable are not too frequent. What makes Ammianus' world so oppressive is the lack of any sort of counterbalance. For if it is true that man is capable of everything horrible, it is also true that the horrible always engenders counter-forces and that in most epochs of atrocious occurrences the great vital forces of the human soul reveal themselves: love and sacrifice, heroism in the service of conviction, and the ceaseless search for possibilities of a purer existence. . . . [Ammianus's] manner of writing history nowhere displays anything redeeming, nowhere anything that points to a better future. [Auerbach, Mimesis, pp. 59–60]

Auerbach has few illusions about the nature of life. It is primarily grim, and certainly the excessive violence and depravity of Ammianus's writing is not what Auerbach disapproves of so strongly. Rather, it is the implication that such writing contains which so disturbs him: that evil may and will occur with rampant profligacy, for no determinable reason, and with no human possibility of influencing its course. To present evil and brutality from a detached position with a subtle, sparse, controlled prose voice: that, perhaps, might be tolerable, for the authorial attitude is reserved. The author's sympathies are not with the cruelty, but could very well be with the victims. To depict evil in an ornate, lush prose, filled with sensual descriptive details, however, is to lovingly dwell in the barbarism, to yield to it with no protest or complaint. This could not be tolerated in Ammianus, for it would deprecate Vico's idea about the history of man or the world of nations. Auerbach had believed that since history was created by man, man could have some role in influencing it, for both the better and the worse. Especially in the midst of the Second World War, he embraced that idea as a security in his attempt to confront the fascist ideology.

If it were true that there was no hope, no possibility for change, then one's life would be worthless, futile; there would be nothing to do but take one's own life or immerse oneself in decadence. Auerbach, despite his inclinations toward a cynical relativism, was too infused with a basic love for humanity: he could not accept the idea of life without hope, and therefore asserted his belief in the ultimate supremacy of "the great vital forces of the human soul." Thus, whenever man's inclinations sink to the very lowest squalor, the "counter-forces" within the spirit of man rise to assert themselves: "love and sacrifice, heroism in the service of conviction, and the ceaseless search for possibilities of a purer existence." This amounts to a mystical assertion of the innate possibilities for goodness in humanity—a belief that Auerbach maintained with urgent desperation during the crisis of war. Faith in the vital forces across history conceivably contradicts Auerbach's earlier notions of historical relativism, but his world and his ideas had been transformed as a result of his forced exile and the new manner of conceptualizing the world which that exile bestowed upon him.

Against the decadent writing of Ammianus with its notion of evil descending upon the world, Auerbach offers the work of St. Augustine with its commitment to Christianity, "itself a movement from the depths." The populist spirit which emerged with the birth of Christianity was temporarily accompanied by the chaos and instability that marked the dissipation of the ancient world and its rigid, lifeless ways. So, for a time, the world was violent and frightening and crude, but at least there was hope. Auerbach thus asserts that the prose of Gregory of Tours—with all its inelegance and lack of craft and dexterity—is admirably realistic: "With Gregory the rigidity is dissolved. He has many horrible things to relate: treason, violence, manslaughter are everyday occurrences; but the simple and practical vivacity with which he reports them prevents the formation of the oppressive atmosphere which we find in the late Roman writers" (Auerbach, *Mimesis,* pp. 69, 94). Therefore, according to Auerbach, the Christian figural interpretive method—infused with the spirit of populism and the cause of the lowly—destroyed the outmoded ancient manner of categorizing the world.

The value of the humanistic outlook of Christianity was partially caused by its existential stance: it simultaneously existed in history and outside of it. Auerbach refers to this quality in what he terms the sublimity of Genesis 1:3; he is impressed by the few words that contain tremendous meanings. But as the years pass and the Church establishes itself as the worldly embodiment of Christ, Auerbach states that the activist basis for figural interpretation declines, the possibility of the Last Judgment and the End of Days becomes less urgent, and the method of figural interpretation becomes in- stitutionalized. For Auerbach, the church is then stodgy, rigid, and elitist (Auerbach, *Mimesis,* pp. 110, 119). Of course, elitism is an- tagonistic to the basic affiliations of Christianity, but as history continues to separate mankind from the incarnation, the Church becomes loftily detached from its strength: the people.

The harsh realities of political government and the decreased dynamism of figural interpretation led, in the early medieval period, to a retreat from realism. What emerged instead was the courtly romance, which was written in a mixture of styles but concerned itself with the affairs of only one social class, the nobility. Its fairy-tale quality was an expression, according to Auerbach, of its attempt to distort life by denying its low elements. The essential lack of function of the nobility was to be seen in their need to idealize love, for they had no real practical or political reason to make life legendary through chivalry unless through the assertion of love as a mystical cause. But behind that lurked a persistent yearning for the sterile securities of a separation of styles like the ancients'; only when the populist roots of

Christianity were weakened could love be offered as a sublime equivalent for Christ (Auerbach, *Mimesis*, pp. 133, 141).

The repercussions of the Fall of the Roman Empire did not last forever. In time, a new stability and order emerged under the bountiful auspices of the now established Church, bolstered by the new tendencies toward nationalism and the consolidation into political states. During that period there was a pervasive movement toward realism because the figural interpretation permeated all aspects of life and because that life had a new continuity as fostered by the Church. The figural interpretation of legend evolved into the figural interpretation of reality, as exemplified by the liturgical plays of the twelfth century. But Auerbach had already implied that the functional existence of the Church as an institution in (or of) the corrupt world worked to erode the dynamic and transcendent populist humanism of the story of Christ and his teachings. The dominance of figural interpretation during that period represented only a movement toward the depiction of everyday realistic life, but the content of Christianity as a vital class-leveling activist unit emerging from the depths of humanity had been lost.

Auerbach now anticipates something else: the secularization of figural realism. But this secularization "does not take place until the frame is broken, until the secular action becomes independent; that is, when human actions outside of Christian world history, as determined by Fall, Passion, and Last Judgment, are represented in a serious vein" (Auerbach, *Mimesis*, p. 160). For Auerbach, only one writer could ever be great enough to utilize the populist mixture of styles in order to create a new sublime style that would surpass the ancients (thus destroying the practical need to emulate their tired notions of categorization) and yet be so magnificent a writer that the sense of detail, imagery, and voice would embrace the present, or historical, sense of existence. Now, as before, that writer is Dante.

Auerbach's discovery of the process of figural interpretation had earlier aided him in his explication of Dante. Through figural in-

terpretation he had gained insight into Dante's historical consciousness and awareness of his use of technique and craft; the use of *figura*
had helped him explain the vivid appeal of Dante's realism within a
supernatural context. Finally, the discussion of figural interpretation
had enabled Auerbach to respond to the political controversy about
race and religion that was current during the 1930s. But these were
now different times and a more critical situation needed to be
addressed. Auerbach could see from Istanbul that if there was one
way in which the ancient literature and fascist popular announce-
ments were related, it was that both resorted to the appeal of legend
and mythology in order to make more grandiose and sublime their
own cause and order. With the war on, and with the Church thus far
having been unable to halt the spread of totalitarian ideology, Auerbach realized that the crucial aspect of Christianity for him was its
origin as a populist movement that had emerged from the lowly
people and had made their concerns and goals important and glori-
ous. It had been an essentially activist movement, vitalized by the
knowledge that the Last Judgment was historically at hand. History
had deprived men of that urgency; instead, the Church prospered as
an institution within the real world. In order to confront ideologies
that depicted themselves as lofty and sublime, one must oppose them
not merely with another lofty alternative (the Church could not
confront the Nazi super Aryan—both were fixed, frozen in doctrine),
but with the lowly themselves, described as seriously (sublimely) as
possible. The contemporary situation insisted on a different interpretation of Dante.

Auerbach brings to his discussion every insight he had cultivated through his years of study; his discussion of the *Comedy*,
on a philological level, is the culmination of his literary work up
to that time. Through specific example after example, he illustrates the functioning of Dante's realism within the frame of the
poem. This time, however, his conclusion is that the dynamic
brilliance of the realistic depictions causes, for the first time, the
figural mode to work effectively within a literary expression; but

then he asserts that the audience's response to the realism supersedes our reaction to the theological base. "In the very heart of the other world," Auerbach says, Dante "created a world of earthly beings and passions so powerful that it breaks bounds and proclaims its independence. Figure surpasses fulfillment, or more properly: the fulfillment serves to bring out the figure in still more impressive relief" (Auerbach, *Mimesis*, p. 200). The effect of the historical figures and their mortal destinies acts to dominate and surpass the effect of the eternal hereafter. This is surely an analysis that contradicts Dante's own express purpose; yet, "Dante's great art carries the matter so far that . . . the beyond becomes a stage for human beings and human passions" (Auerbach, *Mimesis*, p. 201).

Auerbach's focus is now solely upon the realistic elements that Dante had inserted within the eternal context. Earlier he had used his critical resources to explain their effectiveness; in *Mimesis* he analyzes, "as carefully as [he] knows how," the realism in order to assert its predominance over the heavenly sphere (Auerbach, *Mimesis*, p. 219). This assertion is yet another leap from a relativistic position; it can be understood, however, by remembering the historical context that Auerbach is constantly reminding us to maintain. Auerbach is asserting that his response—and our response as readers during the Second World War who are sympathetic to the cause of freedom and egalitarianism—to the realism in Dante is to favor that human sphere above all others, since it is integrally connected to the contemporary crisis of the day. Auerbach writes:

We experience an emotion which is concerned with human beings and not directly with the divine order in which they have found their fulfillment. The eternal position in the divine order is something of which we are only conscious as a setting whose irrevocability can but serve to heighten the effect of their humanity, preserved for us in all its force. The result is a direct experience of life which overwhelms everything else, a comprehension of human realities which spreads as widely and variously as it goes profoundly to the very roots of our emotions, an illumination of man's impulses and passions which leads us to share in them without restraint and indeed to admire their variety and their greatness. And by virtue of this immediate and admiring sympathy with man, the principle, rooted in the divine order, of the indestructibility of the whole historical and individual man turns against that order, makes it subservient to its own purposes, and obscures it. Dante's work made man's Christian-figural being a reality, and destroyed it in the very process of realizing it. [35]

In writing such a passage, he is adopting as activist a literary stance as he can. In times of war and violence we are to seek out in our literature (which is the accumulation through history of our general human quality) those "great vital forces of the human soul" (which are always present in the greatest works of humanistic-realistic art), accept their vigorous affirmation of our humanity—our earthly potentiality—so that, strengthened and rearmed, we can enter our lives anew and ward off the forces that seek to destroy us. The brilliant realism in our greatest literary works should not be absorbed and filed away as credit toward a Last Judgment, but as a dynamic insight into life now within our mortal sphere. The accomplishment of Dante—or rather, Auerbach's assessment of Dante's accomplishment, or better, Auerbach's accomplishment as Dante—is the pivotal key in the movement of Western literature toward humanistic realism. The precedence for a sublimity based on a populist mixture of styles has occurred; the individualized manifestations of the lowly and humble throughout history are the essential transcendent forces of our lives and of our existence as a civilization.

Having invested Dante's style with preeminence in the development of realistic humanism for Western civilization, Auerbach has difficulty relating to Boccaccio, whose work contains remarkable realistic aspects but whose attitude is markedly less pious and serious than Dante's. Auerbach's solution to this problem is to link the realistic tendencies in Boccaccio to his larger philosophy, which he asserts is derived from the ancients: "The *Decameron* develops a distinct, thoroughly practical and secular ethical code rooted in the right to love, an ethics which in its very essence is anti-Christian." This judgment emphasizes the lack of commitment, the superficiality that Auerbach sees as existing outside the Western tradition. What is needed is a realism, after Dante, that can serve "as a basis on which the world could be ordered, interpreted, and represented as a reality and as a whole" (Auerbach, *Mimesis*, pp. 227, 231).

The first steps toward achieving that realism are in the development of a secular populism; Auerbach sees that secularity gestating within Christianity during the late Middle Ages. He refers to this notion as "creaturality," or "life's subjection to suffering and transitoriness." Such an attitude "combines the highest respect for man's class insignia with no respect whatever for man himself as soon as he is divested of them. Beneath them there is nothing but the flesh, which age and illness will ravage until death and putrefaction destroy it. It is, if you like, a radical theory of the equality of all men . . . [based upon] the devaluation of life." The initial basis for this devaluation of life is its diminutiveness when compared with the eternal life of salvation. But, writes Auerbach, the emphasis within creaturality shifts from salvation to the futility of man's life when faced with the horror of his earthly death. By the end of the fifteenth century, the creaturality implicit in the great passion plays had shifted its emphasis to the dreaded realities of life and, especially, death (Auerbach, *Mimesis*, pp. 249–50, 259).

The next functional movement toward humanistic realism in Western literature was also a further transformation of the concept of creaturality. Auerbach isolates these tendencies in the writing of Rabelais. The original idea of the transcendent timeless unity of Christianity led many to believe, by association,

53

that their individual destinies were similarly inviolable. The
mad excess and wild sense of play in the language of Rabelais,
says Auerbach, tempts "the reader out of his customary and
definite way of regarding things, by showing him phenomena in
utter confusion." The reader is forced to confront and "deal
directly with the world and its wealth of phenomena . . . in
Rabelais, creatural realism has acquired a new meaning diamet-
rically opposed to medieval creatural realism—that of the
vitalistic-dynamic triumph of the physical body and its functions." Such a dramatic shift of emphasis to the potentialities of
the human body and the realms of immediate historical earthly
life is a welcome one for Auerbach: the effect can only lead to an
increase in the estimation of our mortal existence. A consequence of considering one's earthly life as important and valuable is to resist and actively struggle against attempts to harm or
malign it. For this reason Auerbach, filled with excitement at the
evolution of his humanistic historical line, terms Rabelais's
populistic mixture of styles "a high style."[36]

Although Auerbach proceeds to analyze his literary texts in
his distinctive meticulous, sensitive, intelligent manner, his
involvement—his subjective feelings of hope as he traces out the
emergence of humanism in Western literature—leads him to
draw larger conclusions that do not always relate to the literary
discussion they follow or the methodology that preceded them.
Thus, Auerbach's concerns are rather transparently on the need
for activist involvement in the contemporary situation and not
on Montaigne as he writes: "But it is also true that his creatural
realism has broken through the Christian frame within which it
arose. Life on earth is no longer the figure of the life beyond; he
can no longer permit himself to scorn and neglect the here for the
sake of a there. Life on earth is the only one he has. He wants to
savor it to the last drop" (Auerbach, *Mimesis,* p. 310). This is a
peculiar passage because both we and Auerbach know (from his
earlier analysis) that life on earth was never solely the figure of

the life beyond; it existed simultaneously in its own historical context that is, Auerbach informed us, a crucial aspect of the figural method of interpretation.

But now Auerbach is concerned with delineating the appearance of a humanistic realism with a consciousness of the unities of history. So he implies here that the figural method is restrictive, nonworldly, just as earlier he had embraced its ability to be both transcendent and historical at once. Increasingly, the political realities intrude on Auerbach's survey because his literary evolution is approaching what he considers the urgent theme, "the highly personal tragedy of the individual" (Auerbach, *Mimesis*, p. 311).

As his allegiance to the individual humanistic realism (which is oriented to the individual and which he believes can effectively oppose the literature of totalitarianism) grew, Auerbach's literary interpretations became progressively radical and summary. Continuing his awkward line of reasoning outlined above, he argues that the Christian view of figural interpretation prohibited the development of the tragic mode (which, to Auerbach, means serious treatment) because the tragedy connected with Christ's life excluded all other secular and individual tragedies. Again, this is a change in emphasis from his earlier assertion that the sublimity of the story of Christ elevated the low subject matter into a populist mixture of styles. In the context of modern literature, however, this is insufficient; Auerbach needs to assert the high tragic depiction of the individual, in order to confront directly the brutal and violent frivolity of totalitarian conceptions of the individual.

The particular aspects of his own contemporary sociopolitical situation help us to appreciate Auerbach's constant larger purpose and conceptualization of his work; thus, the specific interpretations and discussions of modern literature appear less quirky and more of a whole. Auerbach criticizes Shakespeare by saying that he "includes earthly reality, and even its most trivial forms, in a thousand refractions and mixtures, but . . . his purpose goes far beyond the representation of reality in its merely earthly coherence; he embraces reality but he transcends it" (Auerbach, *Mimesis*, p. 327). He is really objecting to Shakespeare's authorial posture of extreme detachment; he wishes there were more activism, more politics, more subjectivity apparent in the plays. From his own historical situation, when one's label, stance, and allegiances are so important, Shakespeare's admirable artistic objectivity is viewed as being morally negligent.

Similarly, Auerbach's potential affinity for the Spanish variants of realism is ruined by his perception that the realism is "fixed" and "immutable"; its representation of reality never confronts any problems or issues, either within its own hermetic society, or in relation to the earthly world. Auerbach senses the increasing urgency of his choices and judgments; for the first time, he allows himself to express a purpose: "In our study we are looking for representations of everyday life in which that life is treated seriously, in terms of its human and social problems or even of its tragic complications" (Auerbach, *Mimesis*, p. 342). Of course, such a statement of purpose could occur only at this point in the study, for it clearly does not apply to many of the earlier works Auerbach dealt with. It does permit him to restrict the possibilities of realism severely to suit his own ideological purpose.

As the historical movement presses more closely on the urgencies of our own reality, Auerbach allows himself to become more caustic, acerbic, and sarcastic. We can see this in his treatment of Cervantes: "It would never have occurred to Cervantes that the style of a novel—be it the best of novels—could reveal the order of the universe . . . so universal and multilayered, so noncritical and nonproblematic a gaiety in the portrayal of everyday reality has not been attempted again in European letters. I cannot imagine where and when it might have been attempted." The implication of the icy tone is that perhaps such a frivolous effort should never have been made in the first place. It is when Auerbach must discuss the emulation and reinstitution—in the France of Louis XIV—of the classical rigid separation of styles that he unleashes his most sardonic criticism. Beneath the controlled outer veneer we can perhaps perceive the militance of Auerbach's concern:

What all these quotations bring out is the extreme exaltation of the tragic personage. Be it a prince who abandons himself to his love in his cabinet . . . or be it a princess going aboard a ship which awaits her . . . the tragic personage is always in a sublime posture, in the foreground, surrounded by utensils, retinue, people, landscape, and universe, as by so many trophies of victory which serve it or are at its disposal. In this posture the tragic personage abandons itself to its princely passions. And the most impressive stylistic effects of this sort are those in which whole countries, continents, or even the universe appear as a spectator, witness, background, or echo of the princely emotions. [37]

For Auerbach believes that it is precisely the arrogance of pompous and destructive tyrants who raise themselves in spurious sublimity, postures of grandeur, that has brought his world to its present state of affairs.

When the fate of humanity hangs in the balance, Auerbach can become moralistic. Thus, he disapproves of the realism in *Manon Lescaut* because it is tinged with an erotic quality: "The pleasure which the author endeavors to evoke in his readers by his representation of his lovers' childishly playful and unprincipled corruption, is in the last analysis a sexual titillation, which is constantly interpreted in sentimental and ethical terms while the warmth it evokes is abused to produce a sentimental ethics" (Auerbach, *Mimesis*, p. 401). And this erotic element is hardly appropriate to the serious treatment of human reality. Similarly, Voltaire's satiric description of the London stock exchange would seem to respond to a variety of critical examinations; but Auerbach uses it only as an opportunity to attack vehemently the propaganda of the Nazis (for Auerbach sees in the dishonest logic of Voltaire the later manipulations of Goebbels). He

57

terms Voltaire's method of description an "impertinence" and con-
demns all "sophists and propagandists" throughout history—
including Voltaire—for their odious and conniving techniques:

*It might be called the searchlight device. It consists in overilluminating one
small part of an extensive complex, while everything else which might
explain, derive, and possibly counterbalance the thing emphasized is left in
the dark; so that the truth is stated, for what is said cannot be denied; and
yet everything is falsified, for truth requires the whole truth and the proper
interrelation of its elements. Especially in times of excited passions, the
public is again and again taken in by such tricks, and everybody knows
more than enough examples from the very recent past. And yet in most
cases the trick is not at all hard to see through; in tense periods, however,
the people or the public lack the serious desire to do so. Whenever a specific
form of life or a social group has run its course, or has only lost favor and
support, every injustice which the propagandists perpetrate against it is
half consciously felt to be what it actually is, yet people welcome it with
sadistic delight.*[38]

What is surprising here is the introduction of the nonrelativistic
term "the whole truth"; more evocatively, we can note an unusual
bitterness in Auerbach's tone as he attempts to account for the
incessant times his sublime-lowly people have been so transparently
duped by malevolent posturing demagogues. The length of the
passage is also telling, and Auerbach is not through with the subject.
He proceeds to present an example of the propaganda device as
described in the work of the Swiss novelist Gottfried Keller (1819–
1890). Keller's analysis is objective and skillful, yet he seems, according to Auerbach, to be a bit too optimistic about the conceivable
positive effects of such propagandistic distortions. Auerbach discusses this buoyancy: "Keller was fortunate in that he could not
imagine an important change of government which would not entail
an expansion of freedom. We have been shown otherwise" (Auerbach, *Mimesis*, p. 404).

Perhaps it is because of his extreme distaste for the nonhumanistic qualities apparent in the literary texts and for the embodiment of these tendencies in the current political situation that Auerbach faces the literary advent of historicism with special eloquence, sensitivity, and grace. He strives for an objectivity; he wishes to convey the impression that he is merely describing the key principles of a historical movement. But his lengthy declaration—phrased entirely in one sentence—and the utopian tone of his passage with its grandeur of language reveal Auerbach's sense of affinity with the movement. The implication is that when the principles of historicism are adopted, then the present age will be viewed properly and the threat destroyed. He calls for societies and historical epochs to be judged by their own premises. These premises are not only natural but intellectual and historical; men must develop a sense of historical dynamics, which includes the belief that historical phenomena are incomparable and have inner mobility. Each individual epoch should be conceived as a unity. The meaning of events can be found not in general forms, but in specific materials, including cultural elements. Finally, the material needed to disclose the meaning will be found "in the depths of the workaday world and its men and women, because it is only there that one can grasp what is unique, what is animated by inner forces, and what, in both a more concrete and a more profound sense, is universally valid" (Auerbach, *Mimesis*, p. 444).

As poignant and animated as the passage is, as vividly as it illustrates Auerbach's concern with affirming what he conceived of as the human quality of life, it must be noted that the statement is contradictory. The notion that one can find "universally valid" materials within the workaday world violates the earlier assertion that we can have no general or absolute truths. Auerbach, in the urgency of his ordeal, has ignored most of the particular methodological principles in the writing of *Mimesis*.

The writers who utilized these ideas—Stendhal and Balzac—are embraced by Auerbach with wholehearted empathy. As we noted earlier, he relates portions of Stendhal's biography and invests his accomplishment with the same aura of heroic innovation that he attributed to Dante. Both Balzac and Stendhal initiated a fiction that represents what Auerbach conceives to be the significant aspects of the reality of Western literature and civilization.

At this point in his text, Auerbach introduces the foundations of modern realism. They should not be strange to us, however, since he has been using them stealthily all along in order to judge phenomena outside of the particular context for the overall purpose of defending these ideals in the first place from the threat of annihilation during the Second World War:

The serious treatment of everyday reality, the rise of more extensive and socially inferior human groups to the position of subject matter for problematic-existential representation, on the one hand; on the other, the embedding of random persons and events in the general course of contemporary history, the fluid historical background—these, we believe, are the foundations of modern realism. [39]

These ideas, in part, are what Auerbach wishes to preserve in the Western civilization; he believes that they are essential to the existence of the civilization, and they are essential to the existence of Erich Auerbach, as well as every individual man. That these principles do not constitute a functional criterion with which to evaluate literary realism Auerbach acknowledges: he admits that most of the realistic works written during the realistic period of the eighteenth century do not satisfy his preconditions. It is equally as evident, however, that the totalitarian doctrine and goals called for the denigration of the qualities Auerbach asserts.

Even within the core of realistic works that he finds to be admirable, Auerbach maintains his reservations. He greatly admires the accomplishment of Flaubert, but is troubled by his apolitical and ultra-art stance: "He sees no solution and no issue; his fanatical mysticism of art is almost like a substitute religion, to which he clings convulsively, and his candor very often becomes sullen, petty, choleric, and neurotic. But this sometimes perturbs his impartiality and that love of his subjects which is comparable to the Creator's love" (Auerbach, *Mimesis*, p. 488). To value anything more highly than one's own humanity and the flowering of humanitarian values throughout our civilization, Auerbach fears, is to risk becoming susceptible to the express notions and ideologies which can destroy that humanity. Still and all, Flaubert's postures do not undermine his brilliantly probing and analytic realism. But Auerbach's reluctance to embrace any writer's emphasis on aesthetic supremacy causes him to devalue many post-Flaubertian realistic works.

In nineteenth century writers, Auerbach finds the work of Emile Zola most notable and profound: his realistic style ignores the trivial urge to entertain his readers and, instead, dwells on the then existing reality, which was ugly and disheartening. Central to his work was the activist theme that called upon the reader to participate in social reform. Zola confronted the greatest issues and problems of his time: "the struggle between industrial capital and labor." He depicted "revolutionary hatred on the verge of breaking out."

Zola took the mixing of styles really seriously; he pushed on beyond the purely aesthetic realism of the preceeding generation; he is one of the very few authors of the century who created their work out of the great problems of the age. . . . If Zola exaggerated, he did so in the direction which mattered; and if he had a predilection for the ugly, he used it most fruitfully. Even today, after half a century the last decades of which have brought us experiences such as Zola never dreamed of, Germinal *is still a terrifying book. And even today it has lost none of its significance and indeed none of its timeliness.*[40]

Here we can see that Auerbach feels the problems of Zola's day have not been effectively solved and remain to disturb the contemporary situation. More important, we can discover, in his enthusiasm, the potentially hazardous idea that when one is asserting the right cause, proceeding from the correct moral outlook and asking the most significant serious questions, certain critical standards of literary evaluation may be compromised in order to incorporate one's admirable goals.

Yet even as Zola achieves an exemplary realistic mixture of styles that Auerbach asserts as a potent weapon against the threat, Auerbach becomes aware of certain other problematic questions which, as he brings his conceptualization of Western literature to a conclusion, intrude to disconcert him. It is as if the detachment that his sociological circumstances in Istanbul provided for him (and with it, the impetus to characterize and interpret the path of Western unity as a whole) falters as the events in history become increasingly familiar to him. So we find Auerbach addressing the peculiar inability of the men and women of the workaday world to recognize the value and greatness and truth of these literary works, now that they have evolved to the level where they embody the worker's—the lowly man's—concerns and dreams. But Auerbach can find no solution, only increasing difficulty. He excuses the workers for not recognizing art since, after working arduously, they require relaxation, not intellectual challenge. He sees, however, that this lack of audience response causes the artist to become increasingly isolated and withdrawn, liable to value his art more than the people who reject him, and thus liable to become elitist, antihumanistic, and aloof.

As Auerbach moves to end his epic survey of Western literature, we can note several points. Throughout the book he has been juggling two contrasting systematic approaches: at times he has been evaluating particular aspects of specific works according to their relativistic and perspectivistic unities. This, of course, is Auerbach's designated approach and he believes that it has been his exclusive method of analysis throughout the book; but as I have attempted to demonstrate, he has also conceived of his survey as a unity, as a generalized interpretation of the history of Western civilization and its literature designed and arranged so that two opposing strands or evolutions appear. The one—rigid, restrictive, categorizing, pompous, elitist, hedonistic, decadent, posturing, and ultimately antihumanity—is meant to be associated with the forces of totalitarianism that were then challenging the fate of the world. The other—fluid, open, populistic, honest, democratic, moral, serious, and ultimately prohumanity—is meant to be associated with the best qualities of the democratic modern Western world.

For Auerbach, the exemplary period of realism is the modern realism of Stendhal, Balzac, and, especially, Zola. Were his survey strictly literary, he would have ended it there. But because his purposes are socio-political as well, he must examine the literature and history of his own era. He attempts it in his final chapter, and in this section the contradictions of his opposing critical approaches emerge: it is, all at once, fussy, frustrating, deeply poignant, and revelatory about Auerbach, the nature of his work, and our civilization.

Auerbach presents and then analyzes a section from Virginia Woolf's novel *To the Lighthouse*. He describes the features of her style and takes exception to them: his point is that since Virginia Woolf is assuming an extremely subjective omniscience (in her characterization of Mrs. Ramsay), for her to retreat from that posture without any explanation in order to make broader observations about Mrs. Ramsay is a manipulation that is dishonest, precious, and antagonistic to the original focus. He objects that Virginia Woolf pretends she— even as the author—is nonomniscient, not the final authority, and that she adopts this pose whimsically and inconsistently. But then he proceeds to explain why Woolf and other modern writers would wish to do this: it is an attempt to be more realistic; it is an attempt to incorporate the modern insight that objective reality can be perceived only through numerous (and fragmented) subjective perceptions. Indeed, the stream of consciousness stylistic technique can be viewed as a means for exploring the inner psychological realms of realism, new territories for representation that were never known to exist previously.

In accordance with his larger conception, Auerbach should appreciate Virginia Woolf. All along, his phrase "mixture of styles" has often meant the mixture of styles and purposes;[41] he should recognize that this new striving to explore inner realms from multitudinous viewpoints in order to achieve a truer realism is a mixture of styles in earnest, a fluidity of conception and a resistance to categorization that is in accord with his larger designations of realism. Surprisingly, Auerbach finds himself resisting these styles, protesting against their formlessness and lack of order. Where earlier he praised the chaotic lack of organization and artistic method in Saint-Simon and the stylistic excesses of Rabelais, he feels threatened by the modernists of his own time (he resorts to his caustic irony about Woolf: "Nothing of importance in a dramatic sense takes place; the problem is the length of the stocking" [Auerbach, *Mimesis*, pp. 421, 539]).

Auerbach finds that he prefers the writing of Marcel Proust; his principal reason is that Proust maintains the consistency and form of a pervasive—albeit highly subjective—first person narrator. His basic dislike of the modern styles seems to be because they lack order, categorization, structure, qualities he had taken to denigrate throughout the study. Again Auerbach demonstrates a real understanding of the characteristic method: he notes that often, "insignificant minor happenings" are presented "for their own sake or rather as points of departure for the development of motifs, for a penetration which opens up new perspectives into a milieu or a consciousness or the given historical setting." There is a shift in emphasis from a tendency to dwell exclusively within decisive historical events or occurrences to capture their significance to the new "confidence that in any random fragment plucked from the course of a life at any time the totality of its fate is contained and can be portrayed" (Auerbach, *Mimesis*, p. 547). In the modern novels, faith is invested in the patterning of exemplary particular events or incidents, instead of attempting to depict exhaustively a chronological evolution or history. Auerbach should have understood this method and procedure, for it is his own critical style.

In the final pages of *Mimesis* Auerbach, in describing the

modernistic rationale for contemporary fiction of his day (of which he disapproved), finds himself describing the critical method he likes to think of himself as using. Naturally, he is aware of this and chooses to discuss it:

It is possible to compare this technique of modern writers with that of certain modern philologists who hold that the interpretation of a few passages . . . can be made to yield more, and more decisive, information . . . than would a systematic and chronological treatment. . . . Indeed, the present book may be cited as an illustration. I could never have written anything in the nature of a history of European realism; the material would have swamped me; I should have had to enter into hopeless discussions concerning the delimitation of the various periods and the allocation of the various writers to them, and above all concerning the definition of the concept realism. . . . As opposed to this I see the possibility of success and profit in a method which consists in letting myself be guided by a few motifs which I have worked out gradually and without a specific purpose, and in trying them out on a series of texts which have become familiar and vital to me in the course of my philological activity; for I am convinced that these basic motifs in the history of the representation of reality—provided I have seen them correctly—must be demonstrable in any random realistic text. [Auerbach, Mimesis, p. 548]*

Auerbach is claiming that his critical work is more accurate and truthful because he developed his motifs out of specific examinations of particular texts, and not out of a futile attempt to absorb all the facts of literary history and make vague conclusions about them. Like the modern novelists, he realizes that "it is a hopeless venture to try to be really complete within the total exterior continuum and yet to make what is essential stand out" (Auerbach, *Mimesis*, p. 548). Of course as a contemporary of those novelists in the same socio-historical context, Auerbach was aware that his ideas about his period would reflect his situation; there would tend to be a similarity of methodology and approach.

Auerbach, however, cannot respond to the writings of his

novelist contemporaries, and as he struggles to perceive the reason for this, we can trace his own reexamination of his own work and his awareness that there is a contradiction. "He who represents the course of a human life, or a sequence of events extending over a prolonged period of time, and represents it from beginning to end, must prune and isolate arbitrarily," Auerbach writes, implying the functioning of a search whose goal is inclusive, generalized truth. However, "there is always going on within us a process of formulation and interpretation whose subject matter is our own self. We are constantly endeavoring to give meaning and order to our lives in the past, the present, and the future, to our surroundings, the world in which we live; with the result that our lives appear in our own conception as total entities" (Auerbach, *Mimesis*, pp. 548–49). Here Auerbach grasps the essential problem in his study. Like his contemporaries, he believes that universal insight can be obtained only from the investigation of particularities within their historical context; the sum total of all particular truths would constitute total truth, but it is impossible to obtain. Instead, as a specific man in a particular place, and possessing a particular and relative perspective, he attempted to "give meaning and order" to his world and his own life; he endeavored to conceive of the elusive world as a "total entity." Believing that the only truth is in the specific, he still imagined a generalized truth because it was impossible for him not to do so.

Auerbach then presents an abbreviated historical summary, detailing the historical factors that would work to popularize and necessitate the use of a relativistic consciousness of life. The confusions of politics and history, the "widening of man's horizon" since the sixteenth century, have led to "crises of adjustment . . . upheavals which we have not weathered yet." And during these intense violent clashes, the historically derived and, therefore, relative ideologies were revealed to be hypocritical, factional, not universal or all-encompassing. But the recognition that the earlier affinities were problematic did not diminish the urge to "entrust oneself to a sect which solved all problems with a single formula, whose power of suggestion imposed solidarity and which ostracized everything which would not fit in and submit." Thus, fascism provided for many of the people a means of resolving and unifying their particularized partial truths, providing fraudulent but comforting answers in the midst of crisis. And it was during that specific historical situation—"at the time of the first World War and after, in a Europe unsure of itself, overflowing with unsettled ideologies and ways of life, and pregnant with disaster "—that the modern writers devised their method of representing reality. That method was "not only a symptom of the confusion and helplessness, not only a mirror of the decline of our world. There is, to be sure, a good deal to be said for such a view." But the reason Auerbach dislikes these novels is that, however correct, they convey "a certain atmosphere of universal doom . . . [leaving] the reader with an impression of hopelessness . . . [they are] turning away from the practical will to live" (Auerbach, Mimesis, pp. 550, 551).

Erich Auerbach had been a writer during those crucial times. Like the others, he had originally yearned for totality, for all-encompassing, generalized values; but the historical conditions had asserted to him the ambiguous nature of universal truth; there could be no absolute truth, but multitudinal, smaller, particularized truths that existed as fragments within the massive society. If the path of history had not then descended on him and, in an existential moment, infused in him the sense of urgency and provided him with the physical and intellectual means of detachment, his specialized, esoteric philological studies would, in their own way, have been a mirror of the deteriorating world situation. But he was seized by the times, propelled through cultures and societies to a vantage point from which he could recognize his task, his historical necessity. Far from producing work that would refer to the truth of its time, his goal was to transcend truth, and thus preserve it.

Auerbach saw himself as one man working both within and apart from a world in the most profound state of upheaval it had ever experienced; one man who knew that ultimate reality was impossible to conceive. The truth was that there could only be an ambiguous mass of fragmented realities: were he to proceed with this insight, both he and the world would perish. In spite of his insight—or perhaps because of it—he labored not to represent reality but to create it, to fashion it anew. His task was to provide humanity with an alternative conception to the one that was threatening the world (a conception which was universal and, therefore, as invalid as its antithesis), an ideal powerful enough to grapple with its enemies and emerge supreme.

Hence Auerbach, close to the end of his mission of affirmation, fervently criticizes and dissects the work of his novelistic contemporaries. The stakes are far too high: their prophecy of doom and hopelessness must be resisted lest it weaken the motivation to struggle against and overcome the antagonistic ideologies. But Auerbach, through his brilliant critical skills, notices a quality of the modern fiction. Auerbach states that the modern writers "put the emphasis on the random occurrence, to exploit it not in the service of a planned continuity of action but in itself" (Auerbach, *Mimesis*, p. 552). Auerbach sees the celebration of the random occurrence not "in the service of a planned continuity of action" (as Auerbach himself is embracing it now in his study) but spontaneously, impulsively (perhaps possible after the war) as the logical heir to the populistic humanism he has been asserting throughout the survey. When the crisis is ultimately resolved, there will emerge something "new and elemental":

nothing less than the wealth of reality and depth of life in every moment to which we surrender ourselves without prejudice. To be sure, what happens in that moment—be it outer or inner processes—concerns in a very personal way the individuals who live in it, but it also (and for that very reason) concerns the elementary things which men in general have in common. It is precisely the random moment which is comparatively independent of the controversial and unstable orders over which men fight and despair; it passes unaffected by them, as daily life. The more it is exploited, the more the elementary things which our lives have in common come to light. The more numerous, varied, and simple the people are who appear as subjects of such random moments, the more effectively must what they have in common shine forth. In this unprejudiced and explor- atory type of representation we cannot but see to what an extent—below the surface conflicts—the differences between men's ways of life and forms of thought have already lessened. . . . Beneath the conflicts, and also through them, an economic and cultural process is taking place. It is still a long way to a common life of mankind on earth, but the goal begins to be visible. And it is most concretely visible now in the unprejudiced, precise, interior and exterior representation of the random moment in the lives of different people. [42]

Having delineated the lines of opposition, Auerbach predicts that the Western strand of literary expression will emerge victorious, and then prevail. Western literature will triumph because it celebrates mixture of styles—the assertion that all humanity is fundamentally linked through our common human-ness, the basic similarity of our goals, interests, lives. The modern novels are an aspect in this posi- tive trend because they emphasize the random moment, and the random moment is independent from the suspicious ravages of politics; it is what all men have in common and it will weather all crises. Already, perhaps, a peaceful community of man has been conceived: "Below the surface conflicts—the differences between men's ways of life and forms of thought have already lessened. . . . It is still a long way to a common life of mankind on earth, but the goal begins to be visible." This is the light at the end of the tunnel for Auerbach, the resolution of the crisis, the goal toward which he has been working, interpreting the literatures of Western civilization. It is the ultimate political consequence of the humanistic ideals that will survive the totalitarian threat.

Erich Auerbach realizes, at the very end of the enormous study, that the peaceful common existence of mankind is not a dream to anticipate fervently, but a dreary sentence of which one should be wary. He fears that the future of man will not be communal, but common in the coarsest sense; the society that survives the crisis will be populistic, but also undifferentiated. It will be not only elementary, but hopelessly simplistic. The enormity of his insight fills him with despair:

So the complicated process of dissolution which led to fragmentation of the exterior action, to reflection of consciousness, and to stratification of time seems to be tending toward a very simple solution. Perhaps it will be too simple to please those who, despite all its dangers and catastrophes, admire and love our epoch for the sake of its abundance of life and the incomparable historical vantage point it affords. But they are few in number, and probably they will not live to see much more than the first forewarnings of the approaching unification and simplification.[43]

In the closing lines of his text—the work of unifying synthesis he has been composing in urgency and courageous affirmation—Auerbach discovers that he is only a man *in* time. Just as in the work of his contemporaries—Joyce, Woolf, Proust, Mann, Gide—we find in these lines "a certain atmosphere of universal doom." He had written of the modernists: "We not infrequently find a turning away from the practical will to live, or delight in portraying it under its most brutal forms" (Auerbach, *Mimesis*, p. 551). He finds that, like the novelists whose work he dislikes but whose history he shares, his love is for the society in crisis and turmoil; when faced with the possibility of living in a peaceful, simplified future, he anticipates his own death. The end of *Mimesis*, like *To the Lighthouse*, "breathes an air of vague and hopeless sadness."

With the completion of *Mimesis*, Auerbach understood that he had been the urgent and militant champion, not of an ideal goal, but of a dynamic process. He had condemned the modern writers of fiction, yet methodologically he saw himself as one of them. He had devoted the work to an assertion of the populist unities—mixture of styles, serious treatment of low characters and subjects—that link man to man, culture to culture, only to find that the initial manifestation of those ideals was an expression of randomness, undifferentiation, simplicity, all of which he found intolerable. He had invested one strand of literature with absolute positive qualities; outside of their particularized contexts, projected into an idealized future, they were horrific, frightening. Auerbach concluded, reluctantly and with sadness, that his own critical writing was not of a piece with the literature he wished to interpret and celebrate.

In another sense, however, his work was linked to the others: they were all products of their historical period and premises. Odd as it might seem, Auerbach's primary affinity was toward the evocation of the moment that is simultaneously eternal: the act of writing one's history as past while living it as present occurrences; the sense of creating an art that is absolute and permanent while enduring the process of corporeal deterioration and death; the inclination to live away from society and also within; the fragile and existential realm-in-common between the societies of literary eternity and the turbulent, everchanging, fluid society of now.

In the months between the completion of *Mimesis* and the end of the Second World War, Auerbach undoubtedly thought long and hard about his work and the conflicting forces embodied within it. Probably there was the urge to revise portions in order to improve the symmetry, achieve a greater unity. But with the world at peace, the urgency for him to wage ideological war was diminished. Auerbach had produced an enormous, brilliant work that was partially relevant to present concerns (the movement to return to secular literary studies) and partially irrelevant to the contemporary notions of peace and reconstruction (the resonances about two hostile evolutions of literature were certainly not attuned to a world eager to forget the immediate past).

With the world at peace, Auerbach returned once more to the concept of historical relativism, although his thoughts were pervaded with the same cynical sadness that had characterized the final section of *Mimesis*. His work and his life were both a product of the times; so, in order to appreciate *Mimesis*, one needed always to remember the context, the circumstances of its creation. Unless one were to link his

71

ideas with the history that had shaped them, the book would seem problematic and perplexing. Whether ultimately viewed as good or bad, the most important evaluation was that *Mimesis* was the only work Erich Auerbach could have written from his situation and historical perspective. The book was completed and consigned to history. Auerbach turned his attention to other concerns, the most personal being his decision to emigrate to the United States.

In 1947, Auerbach took a leave of absence from the University of Istanbul and journeyed to the United States with his wife, Marie and son, Clemens. After receiving an appointment as visiting professor of Romance languages at Pennsylvania State College, he decided to remain permanently. Many aspects of the move no doubt appealed to Auerbach: for the first time in twelve years he would enjoy the benefits of excellent library facilities, serious and challenging students, and a scholarly environment in which he could work. At fifty-five years of age, and after a decade of hard work (he had released not only *Mimesis* in 1946, but *Neue Dantestudien* in 1944),[44] it would certainly have been pleasant for him to resume his careful and detailed philological studies in a leisurely manner. For many European scholars the end of the war and the new opportunities in the United States were the means to thrust the past behind them and return to their esoteric academic work. But not all of them had made the compelling attempt at synthesis that was *Mimesis*, not all of them were concerned with linking their scholarship to their current surroundings, not all of them possessed the complex mind of Auerbach.

For Auerbach, the move to the United States was still another movement through societies; and as his past transportation to Istanbul had enabled him to examine Europe, so his arrival in the United States provided him with the detachment to examine the work and conclusions he conceived of in Turkey about Western Europe. It was a time to attempt some resolution of the contradictions he sensed in *Mimesis*, or, if not a resolution, then a clarification. But for the rest of his life his experience and thoughts would be tinged with ambiguity.

First of all, for the first time in his life he possessed the means and

opportunity to lead a productive and serene scholarly life. His work
was known to American scholars, and he was granted considerable
prestige and treated with courtesy and respect. But just as life became
more bountiful, he was forced to consider death. Auerbach was
unable to assume a tenured position at Pennsylvania State because
the required medical examination disclosed a heart condition.[45] He
spent the next year as a member of the Institute for Advanced Study
at Princeton. In 1950 he was named professor at Yale University; he
remained at Yale for the rest of his life.

Concomitantly, his work was receiving considerable critical attention. The original German edition of *Mimesis* was available in the
United States; the individual chapters of the book in English translation were beginning to appear in the American literary journals.
Auerbach, in addition, was contributing new work to the journals,
written in English—book reviews, sketched fragments, minute
pieces on Dante. The critical response to *Mimesis* was, for the most
part, highly complimentary and many of the writers devoted considerable space to praising the remarkable variety and breadth of Auerbach's work.[46] But the comparative complacency of the times was
such that the critics discussed and evaluated Auerbach's work as if it
were the leisurely, quiescent, culminating work of an elderly scholar's serene career; there was hardly an attempt made to examine the
survey from the historical context Auerbach had suggested and the
socio-political conditions he had repeatedly alluded to. Instead, the
aptness and brilliance of Auerbach's specific observations were
praised, but there was general perplexity and disagreement about the
work's unity. Repeatedly, critics were unable or unwilling to draw
distinctions between Auerbach's specific literary focal points and the
larger, more expansive political and historical illuminations he con-
structed around them.

We can gain insight into Auerbach's reaction to the critical evaluations of his book by briefly examining his review of another book.
Ernst Robert Curtius was one of the few European scholars of equivalent stature to Auerbach; he, too, considered himself a Romance

philologist. But during the war he had been able to remain in Germany with access to the archives and libraries necessary for his work. The result of this scholarship was *Europäische Literatur und lateinisches Mittelalter*, another massive book.[47] Curtius, however, was concerned with demonstrating the unity of Western literature and culture from antiquity to the present, focusing on the Latin language as the unifying element. Where Auerbach had been partisan and militant, Curtius was universal and beneficent; more direct than Auerbach, he referred to his work as an attempt to preserve Western culture and humanism. For Curtius, the war was a tragedy, but then and now, we are all one: we share a united culture.

In Auerbach's review we can isolate his resentment through his cultivated and subtle ironies: "It is well known that Mr. Curtius represents a unique combination of scholarship and modern literary background, of largeness of horizon and philological accuracy, of commonsense and refinement; it may be added that this work, *planned and executed in Germany, roughly between 1932 and 1947*, is a monument of powerful, passionate and *obstinate* energy"[48] (My italics). Auerbach here feels the need to assert the same facts and location of composition for Curtius as he had provided for himself in *Mimesis*. He praises Curtius's scholarship, but refers to the "overwhelming abundance" of particular scholarly details to the point that the "leading ideas" become "blurred." Auerbach's design was to place both works back into the historical context from which they emanated: the result would assert the quality of Auerbach's own intentions and contribution while revealing Curtius as a vaguely suspicious defender of Western humanism.

Auerbach's last years were spent in the United States. During that time he attempted to consolidate the various elements and affinities of his literary and historical writings into a coherent, functional unity. This meant that he had to reinterpret his past interpretations of literary history so that they would suit the present context. At the same time, he wished to defend and fortify the original (and ultimate) correctness of his earlier statements. The result was that Auerbach tried to encompass positions that seemed contradictory; frequently he would renounce an idea, only to assert it again in a more subtle mode.

In the United States he was granted the means for a comfortable and fruitful life; it was also revealed to him that his death was a real and imminent possibility. These opposing impulses and extremities characterized his last writings. The conflict of the Second World War was over, but he had discovered in *Mimesis* that the solution to the crisis—a peaceful, common life of mankind—was, for him, another crisis. Sadly, and with profound cynicism, he had reflected that his own yearnings were for the literature and ideas that had helped foster the recent destructive war. He felt that the criticism of *Mimesis* indicated an attempt to distort the original and significant basis of his thesis. If only the book could be viewed as the work of a particular man addressing special historical circumstances at a distinct moment of history, then his meanings and designs would be clearly evident.

At the same time he began to feel sorry that he had ever, in *Mimesis*, formulated any "general expressions" in the first place. It would have been better, he wrote, had he only provided specific and particular textual examples of his ideas, hoping that the reader would, by accumulating all the specific instances, gain insight into the nature of the unity Auerbach would have had in mind all along but never directly expressed.[49] Of course he never actually believed that it was possible to delineate the whole through a subjective accumulation of the parts (we discussed earlier his aversion to this idea), but such was the extent, he felt, of the critical misconstruction of his work, such was the extent of his postwar mournfulness that he ironically suggested that it would have been preferable for him to have formulated no abstract theories at all rather than to have his themes and ideas so patently misunderstood.

Beneath this melodramatic declaration, Auerbach was carefully reading his critics: they had noted that certain periods had been skipped over, had received no attention. Perhaps if he completed similar studies of the periods he had left out of *Mimesis*, the individual weight of his evidence would reinforce his original ideas and convince the skeptics. With that in mind, he began work upon *Literatursprache und Publikum in der lateinischen Spätantike und im Mittelalter*, a volume he conceived as "a supplement to *Mimesis*," but without "the loose but always perceptible unity of *Mimesis*"— reflecting, however, the same "singleness of purpose."[50]

Hence, *Literary Language and Its Public* may be approached as a work that continues the investigation of *Mimesis*, but without the political urgency of that earlier work, conceived and produced during years of crisis and antagonism. According to Auerbach, *Mimesis* had been misinterpreted partly as a result of a failure by critics and general readers to regard its spirited and militant assertion of Western humanistic values as being relative to its historical context of strife and turmoil. Now, in an age of peace, yet with the threat of rampant cultural undifferentiation a distinct possibility, Auerbach believed that it ought to be possible to reflect the same singleness of purpose without the imposing assertiveness that he thought had been mandated by the war years. *Literary Language and Its Public*, therefore, was meant "to be read as a whole," but "is a fragment or rather a series of fragments," because of his deliberate decision to suppress "the loose but always perceptible unity of *Mimesis*" in order to better suit his conception of the sensibility of the day. Since Auerbach intended for *Literary Language and Its Public* to fill the "number of obvious gaps [in *Mimesis*]," the process of reestablishing Auerbach's work in its historical context will contribute to our ability to sense the unity behind *Literary Language and Its Public* and see it as a work that perpetuates the humanistic and populistic themes of *Mimesis* in a quieter tone of voice for a more subdued and less individualistic age. Its great significance and value for critical literature are apparent. As a work in praise of historical change, its reception by its audience must serve as a function of that history: thus, Auerbach hoped for "readers [who] will help in the search . . . ; by giving more precise and effective expression to what I have tried to say, [one of them] will find the theme."[51]

Auerbach's final writings suggest another connotation as well. At the end of *Mimesis*, he had suggested that the new age of peace and humanity would be sterile and undifferentiated; this world-weary attitude was intensified in the late works and Auerbach expressed it in increasingly desolate terms. His thought and expressions were pervaded by a spectral tonality, an intimation that the world would soon end (or, if not the world, then the historical process as we had known it and, with it, all historical perspective, to be replaced by a dreary and static leveling-off of categories and gradations). The reluctant and qualified activism of the earlier works was transformed in the United States into a spirited and vocal seclusiveness.

But how can the sense of impending doom be reconciled with the great amount of research and writing Auerbach produced in his last decade of life? Certainly Auerbach wanted to convey the impression that the slings and arrows of critical misreadings were forcing him out of the muddied arena of contemporary political history and into the unsullied, purer realms of ancient and medieval literary philology. At the same time that Auerbach sincerely feared the imminent end of the historical process and historical perspectivism, this predicted cessation provided, ultimately, the unqualified absolute that was required for him to believe that his ideas were not merely correct for their historical time, but absolutely correct, for they were formulated at the culmination of all historical time.

The transformation of Auerbach's emphasis and purpose can be clearly ascertained through a brief glimpse of a few of his later articles. Auerbach wrote "Der Triumph des Bösen, Versuch über Pascals politische Theorie," in 1946. It was translated into English after Auerbach's emigration and appeared as "The Triumph of Evil in Pascal."[52] Both of Auerbach's versions of the article were concerned with many philological questions: he presents a logical explication of Pascal's text in *Pensées* to demonstrate Pascal's development of the notion that might is right, not ironically, but intrinsically. He also discusses the political and historical circumstances of the Port-Royal theological controversy in order to explore the conception of Pascal's extreme critique of secular life. Auerbach demonstrates that behind the militant condemnation of the transient earthly world was a complete acquiescence to the political institutions and powers of the secular world.

Auerbach's larger purpose here was to imply a parallel between the Church, long separated from its historical-populistic germination—a secular, political power in its own right—and the lofty, arbitrary, and oppressive political powers who initiated the Second World War. Both called upon their adherents to subjugate and negate assertions of their own humanity and existence in order to preserve and protect the political institutions that would enslave them. But the shift in allegiance—from the spiritual higher cause to the corrupt earthly power—was stealthily contained in the standard language of religious observation. Without even realizing the subtle change, a sincerely devout individual might act to enforce the political power that oppresses him. The point was to explore the mentality and psychology of the European peoples who had allowed the recent fascist states to ensnare them for quite a while, and who, even now, were permitting the emergence of Communist totalitarian states. Part of the key to their acceptance, Auerbach proposed, was that the significant meaning of the threat was wrapped and hidden in official language, proclamations of statutes and ordinances, which are outside the scope of most people's attentions. The emphasis, again, was to embrace the active movements of the lowly people and condemn the lofty secular institutional powers.

But in the same year as his English translation, Auerbach was revising and expanding his article for permanent inclusion in book form: it would appear as "Über Pascals politische Theorie" in *Vier Untersuchungen zur Geschichte der französischen Bildung* and as "On the Political Theory of Pascal" in *Scenes from the Drama of European Literature*.[53] Although all of the articles are antagonistic to the mechanisms by which someone would view might as pure evil but, out of a "higher" allegiance, assert it to be right and inviolable on earth, the earlier pieces are more heavily ironic, infused, to a greater degree, with Auerbach's earlier activist involvement. By the time he revised the articles, he was concerned with the deterioration of the Western world, worried about the leveling process that he feared would eliminate all cultures, languages, literatures, history.

In the later pieces, he removed much of the virulence and the direct political implications (especially in the title). He also added some new material, much of it unusual. For instance, he interprets original sin as "the inextricable fabric of heredity, historical situation, individual temperament, and the consequences of our own actions, in which we are everlastingly involved." This reconception is consistent with Auerbach's substitution of the flow of history for the doctrine of Christianity as the ultimate cause. But here he uses it to assert that "anyone who succeeds in recognizing that whatever happens to him is just, regardless of how wrong others may have been in doing it, has, it seems to me, not only acquired a foundation for ethical attitude, but has also found a new way of looking at everything that happens in the world."[54] This is a notion that is, at once, filled with stoic resignation, transcendental vision, and ascetical yearnings; they are the words of a man who hoped that he "probably [would] not live to see much more than the first forewarnings of the approaching unification and simplification."

We can detect further evidence of Auerbach's inclinations in his article "Baudelaires Fleurs du Mal und das Erhabene," which appeared in English as "The Aesthetic Dignity of the 'Fleurs du Mal.' "[55] Auerbach, perhaps prophetically, described this article as his farewell to modernity.[56] We may recall that several years earlier, in Istanbul, Auerbach had condemned Ammianus's graphic depiction of horrendous, morbid, and grotesque aspects of life because Ammianus presented a caricature of life; nowhere did Ammianus "display anything redeeming, anything that points to a better future." Now, in the United States, he refers to the symbolic images of Baudelaire as "extremely realistic," because "they forcefully concretize a hideous and terrible reality."[57] Auerbach feels a great deal more empathy with the hopeless despair of Baudelaire than with the similar feelings in Ammianus: Baudelaire "wrote in the grand style about paralyzing anxiety, panic at the hopeless entanglement of our lives, total collapse—a highly honorable undertaking, but also a negation of life." Baudelaire's writing, then, is "a negation of life," but is yet "extremely realistic." Such an idea is already a contradiction of the terminology and ethic Auerbach used in *Mimesis* to assert the need for activist involvement, but to assert the "aesthetic dignity" of Baudelaire's style is to alter more profoundly the earlier critical proposals. Auerbach's reason for that designation was his belief that Baudelaire "disclosed something that was latent in his age" (Auerbach, *Scenes*, pp. 208, 220).

Earlier we have seen how Auerbach had rejected that philosophy of realism as the revelation of the true nature of a historical period when he had criticized Ammianus; but then, of course, he had been writing to preserve the humanity of Western civilization. Now he believes that by saving humanity he has helped to destroy the dynamic of history and the movement of life.

So Auerbach, in the United States, felt himself to be trapped within a threatening, unyielding world: a world in which the humanistic tendencies had been carried so far that the qualities of existence were vanishing—life itself was becoming undifferentiated. It is no wonder that his conception of realism changed to include Baudelaire, for whom "there is no way out, nor can there be." It is no wonder that his perspective on life changed to the extent that he was receptive to the existentialism of Jean-Paul Sartre (whose introduction to Baudelaire's *Ecrits intimes* [Paris, 1946] Auerbach regarded as "brilliant" and whom he considered "an acute and concrete thinker though his designs obtrude too much"). For, to Auerbach, the current crisis of our civilizations was described by Baudelaire in its latent form. The human structure that appeared in Baudelaire's work had been a significant influence in the development of contemporary poetry and all the other literary genres of the modern day: "the trace of Baudelaire's influence can be followed in Gide, Proust, Joyce, and Thomas Mann as well as Rimbaud, Mallarmé, Rilke, and Eliot."

Baudelaire's accomplishment was to "concretize" the world as it was; his literary descendants intensified his effort. Together, they depicted the human structure that was influential in the current "transformation, or perhaps one should say the destruction of the European tradition." According to Auerbach, "Baudelaire's style, the mixture we have attempted to describe, is as much alive as ever" (Auerbach, *Scenes*, pp. 220, 225, 223).

Considering Auerbach's estimation of his contemporary society, it is not difficult to appreciate his desire to return to more historically removed periods of historical philology. Nor is it hard to appreciate why, after being named to the prestigious position of Sterling Professor at Yale in 1956, he took a leave of absence to visit Europe. When viewing Europe in 1956, with sad awareness of the approaching anesthetization of its cultures, he no doubt conceived it not as the scarred and torn landscape of recent violence, but rather as the birthplace—and perhaps the resting place—of the dynamic, life-affirming philosophy of history he relished above all else. During his visit he received the honors and praise that had eluded him earlier in his life.

The following year, having completed his scholarly examination of medieval literature for the book that would be the supplement to *Mimesis*—a further affirmation of the literary style and conception of life he felt was now doomed—Auerbach decided to summer in Germany. It was there that he suffered what he thought was a slight stroke, and on his return to the United States he still suffered the effects. He entered a Connecticut sanitarium to rest and recover. He died there on October 13, 1957.

In the epilogue to *Mimesis*, Auerbach wrote that he hoped to find readers for his work. Since his death, his contribution has helped to expand the scope and purpose of all subsequent literary investigations; he has inspired many readers to think spiritedly about relative generic conceptual categories for literature. His notion that literary evolution was a coherent and fluid movement has influenced current conceptions of literary structure as a system.

In this effort to discuss Auerbach and his work from the context of the significant historical and sociological factors which affected them, I have tried to demonstrate that Auerbach's intentions went beyond the purely literary. In a time of crisis and fluctuation, his resolve was to renovate the priorities and values of Western civilization and thus preserve them. In his attempt, he struggled to unify essentially incompatible concepts of absolute morality and extreme relativism. If the result was less than totally successful, it matters less than the nature of his design: he sought to advance the positive historical impetus of man's creative energies. Perhaps the quotation from Montaigne of which he was fond is also applicable to Erich Auerbach and the works of his lifetime: "The undertaking smacks of the quality of what it has in view; for the striving is a good part of the result, and consubstantial with it" (Auerbach, *Scenes*, p. 223).

Leo Spitzer

The death of Leo Spitzer in 1960 marked the end of literary historical studies in Romance philology as practiced by the four great European scholars—Auerbach, Curtius, Vossler, and Spitzer. So broad and extensive was the range of Spitzer's intellectual activities that many critics felt it would be impossible to assess his contribution fully. Even René Wellek, whose grasp of Spitzer's work was considerable, held that "it will be difficult to find a person adequate to the task" of evaluating Spitzer's life and works. Such an individual, Wellek noted, would have to be a linguist in Romance languages, a literary historian with an expansive realm of expertise from antiquity to the present, a general historian of ideas, and a literary critic and theorist.[1] In effect, all meaningful appraisals of Spitzer ought to be suspended until a younger Spitzerian double might be found: such has been the state of our understanding of Spitzer two decades after his death.

This general reluctance to deal with Spitzer has been intensified by the fact that Spitzer (to use Wellek's phrase) "had little interest in composing his own papers and did not write a single unified book . . . [he] was convinced that his own position can be best defined by relating it to that of others, by distinguishing, defining, and redefining."[2] Thus, our perception of Spitzer's work has been that it would constitute a whole on the basis of its accumulated components, once a person was found who would be able to undertake such a task. Since Spitzer did not seem to be concerned with producing a unified body of work, it was assumed that he lacked a holistic perspective, that each particular critical act was isolated and not concerned with an authorial thematic consistency. Since Spitzer devoted a good deal of effort to positioning his ideas in relation to his scholarly contemporaries, it was assumed that he was a critic of surfaces, that he was content to survey the field of academic achievement with only an occasional original contribution that was not based on another's ideas.

Such an approach to Spitzer's work is misguided, I believe: it conceives of Spitzer as an extraordinarily talented intellectual dilettante rather than as a scholar with several skills and interests who believed in the intrinsic affinity of humanistic realms. It ignores Spitzer's interest in the "web of interrelations between language and the soul of the speaker." Although he granted that "each single essay is intended to form a separate, independent unit," he asserted that "the repetitions of theoretical and historical statements which are the unavoidable consequence of this manner of presentation will be felt by the reader rather as recurrent *leitmotifs* or *refrains* destined to emphasize a constancy and unity of approach."[3]

But what sort of thematic unity might we derive from a huge number of occasional pieces devoted to an equally vast array of subjects and disciplines? An answer would necessarily include Spitzer's awareness that literary and intellectual activities were not isolated or self-contained, but required an interactive relationship between an author and his public: "For poetry has always been addressed to a public with which the poet felt himself to be united—so that the explanation of poetry, too, must needs be addressed to a public whose reactions the commentator is able to foresee."[4] The literary critic must be concerned, initially, with an author's text and the way in which that author's assessment of his literary public affected that text; further, he must concentrate on the audience which influences his own work about that literary text emanating from an earlier author-public interaction. This orientation—that every literary act is also reactive, that a larger, time-centered context surrounds all creative activity—is an essentially historical one, but by no means does it reflect a conventional sense of historical understanding.

Spitzer's elucidation of his own conception of the critical function is as follows:

It is one of the benefits falling to the lot of the emigrant scholar that, however much his outward activity may be curtailed in the new country in comparison with his former situation, his inner activity is bound to be immensely enhanced and intensified: instead of writing as he pleases, after the usual fashion of the German scholar in particular (who is so well satisfied to live in the paradise of his ideas, whether this be accessible to his fellow men or not), he must, while trying to preserve his own idea of scholarship, continually count with his new audience, bearing in mind not only the conventional requirements but also those innermost strivings of the nation (inasmuch as it is given him to feel them) which, opposed to his nature as they may have seemed to him in the beginning, tend imperceptibly to become a second nature in him—indeed, to make shine by contrast his first nature in the clearest light.[5]

A change has been described here, an alteration of his idea of criticism that coincides with his change of nationality. As a Viennese philologist, he had been content to "live in the paradise of his ideas"—self-absorbed, detached from society—producing scholarly works not "accessible to his fellow men." As an American, his task becomes more complex: he must "preserve his own idea of scholarship," that is, maintain his distinctly European humanistic world view and philological method. In addition, he must address his new audience and American public, assessing not only the "conventional requirements" of his society, but gauging, somehow, the "innermost strivings of the nation" and reflecting that ideal. The texts that are produced in this manner will concern both the past and the future. They will chronicle one man's process of assimilation from a Viennese fin de siècle ethos of creative intellectual detachment to a peculiarly American sense of moral obligation and democratic community. But as the culture (and academic attitude) of one country was at first perceived by the critic as being opposed to the culture of the other country, so the critic—now in harmony with his new nation—will articulate a perpetuity of confrontational positions melding into unity. Such a formulation suggests a history given cogency by the encompassing faculties of a human sensibility—one that exists in time and addresses the timeless, one that represents, in the language of literary history, the path of an intuited moral consciousness. It is a history in which the past is a presence within a process of critical enunciation that forges the future of our shared cultural sensibility.

Another factor contributing to the reticent attitude about Spitzer's work is the difficult nature of his writing style: "Spitzer tucks away important materials and ideas in long footnotes, and there are often footnotes to footnotes"[6]—and this in the five languages in which he wrote fluently (German, French, Italian, Spanish, and English). Might this not limit his ability to be "accessible to his fellow men"? To the extent that we have been waiting for a new Spitzer in order to understand the old one, this has certainly been the case. But it is not evident that Spitzer desired this difficulty: as we shall see, he often modified his manner of presentation, depending on his anticipated audience and his subject matter.

To one for whom "language is only one outward crystallization of the 'inward form,' or, to use another metaphor: the lifeblood of the poetic creation is everywhere the same, whether we tap the organism at 'language' or 'ideas,' at 'plot' or at 'composition,' " an involuted, multireferential mode of presentation may serve as the "outward crystallization" through which we are meant to penetrate to the "inward form" of the "soul of the speaker." Further, since Spitzer believed that "the best document of a nation is its literature, and since the latter is nothing but its language as this is written down by elect speakers," and that we may "grasp the spirit of a nation in the language of its outstanding works of literature,"[7] it may be proposed that his expression in many languages is one way to "tap" his "lifeblood" of Western humanism; that his works in English represent his conception of the historical spirit and soul of the United States during his lifetime.

Our history is documented by our literature, which is itself the transcription of language by "elect speakers." Certainly, such a construction calls for an inquiry into the nature of the elect speakers—are they an intellectual elite, especially able to penetrate to the spirit of a nation? And if so, how are the characteristics of this group determined? Spitzer's suggestion is that a critic's functional artistic capacity is

deeply anchored in the previous life and education of the critic, and not only in his scholarly education: in order to keep his soul ready for his scholarly task he must have already made choices, in ordering his life, of what I would call a moral nature: he must have chosen to cleanse his mind from distraction by the inconsequential, from the obsession of everyday small details—to keep it open to the synthetic apprehension of the "wholes" of life, to the symbolism in nature and art and language.[8]

At first glance, this might appear to resemble the extreme historical relativism of an Auerbach: the most a critic can do is to make judgments about history that result from his previous life and education. Our knowledge of the present is dependent on our present circumstances—and as these are altered, so are our historical evaluations. But Spitzer was always sensitive to the limitation of such a stance; he proposes that "there is one inconsistency in nineteenth-century historicism: that, wholly given up to historical relativism, it has not yet learned to see the relativity of its own procedures, conditioned by certain definite events of modern history; and that it has not learned to take itself as a historical fact, subject to change. Before itself, it ceases to think historically."[9] Thus, it becomes clear that Spitzer's conception is of a uniquely motivated critic, one who is "ordering his life" to be able to delve to the "inward form," one who makes "choices" of "a moral nature," so that he may be deemed fit to attain an awareness of "those innermost strivings of the nation." As part of his purification rites, he "cleanse[s] his mind from distraction by the inconsequential, from the obsession of everyday small details," in order to rise to a "synthetic apprehension of the 'wholes' of life."

To properly comprehend this equation of secular critical acuity with religious spiritual purity, we need to clarify the occasion for Spitzer's statement. Accordingly, I think it is evident that Spitzer is not here prescribing qualities for an idealized critic or group of critics; rather, he is describing himself and his own spiritual and intellectual development. To place oneself as the arbiter of a historical representation of moral truth through literary form is an uncommon position to take, and it is worthwhile to inquire about whether there is evidence for such a stance in Spitzer's elaboration of his critical procedure, or method.

Spitzer's method (or, as he preferred, "habitual procedure of the mind") centers on an intuitive "inner click" of understanding, by which the critic—in a revelatory instant of insight—comes to perceive the intrinsic order of a work of literature ("the parts aggregating to a whole, time filled with contents"). Next, the critic proceeds deductively in order to establish—through textual evidence—the accuracy of his initial assumption. Making several "to and fro voyages" between the surface of a work of art and its "inward life-center," he arrives at a state of certainty that either his preliminary intuition was correct, or else that it was misguided. Spitzer referred to his method as "the philological circle" and as the "circle of understanding," based on Fr. D. E. Schleiermacher's notion "that cognizance in philology is reached not only by the gradual progression from one detail to another detail, but by the anticipation or divination of the whole"—influenced, as well, by the work of Wilhelm Dilthey and Gustav Gröber.[10]

A persistent question that accompanies Spitzer's philological circle is, namely, Why does an intuitive assumption about a literary text (an inner click) often lead to a profound understanding of the inner unity of a work of art, which can then be verified through textual evidence? Spitzer's answer: that he "know[s] of no way to guarantee either the 'impression' or the conviction . . . . : they are the results of talent, experience, and faith." It is here that we encounter the determinism of the critic's previous life and educational experience, but that is not all. There is talent as well. This talent may be obtained through practice ("the 'click' will come oftener and more quickly after several experiences of 'clicks' have been realized by the critic"), but practice may not be sufficient: "even then, it is not a foregone conclusion that it will inevitably come; nor can one ever foretell just when and where it will materialize." How can one avoid being arbitrary or indulgent in one's choice of intuitive hypothesis? "The reader must seek to place himself in the creative center of the artist himself and re-create the artistic organism." In effect, the critical reader must subjugate himself and his individual will to the wonder of form that is the literary work of art. If he is sufficiently energetic and humble and makes the appropriate choices of a moral nature, then he may have attained a satisfactory state of purity so that his instinctive sense impressions will pierce to the heart of the artist's truth. He must rely on "the feeling, which we must have already acquired, for the whole of the particular work of art" (Spitzer, *Linguistics and Literary History*, pp. 27–29). So we move from experience, to talent, to faith.

Spitzer's reliance on impulse, intuition, and faith often provoked the criticism of his philological circle that it is a "vicious circle." The inner click, accordingly, does not provide a hypothesis that is then evaluated according to objective evidence from the text; rather, it offers a contrived context by which the literary text is subjectively distorted in order to prove that which was the hypothesis and method simultaneously. Spitzer's answer to such arguments is that "the first step, on which all may hinge, can never be planned: it must already have taken place." There is a distinction to be made between the reason and rigor that regulate the objective analysis of the text in order to verify the click, and the click itself, which remains spiritual: "How can we say when exactly it began? (Even the 'first step' was preconditioned.) We see, indeed, that to read is to have read, to understand is equivalent to having understood." Further, Spitzer compares this philological process to "the way followed by the theologians who start from on high, to take the downward path toward the earthly maze of detail." Indeed, Spitzer proposes that his philological circle defies the ability of our critical resources to understand it: "The solution attained by means of the circular operation cannot be subjected to a rigorous rationale because, at its most perfect, this is a negation of steps: once attained, it tends to obliterate the steps leading up to it" (Spitzer, *Linguistics and Literary History*, pp. 26, 27, 23, 26).

In truth, Spitzer is not attributing a systematic order to his stylistic criticism—a consistent procedure that may be explained, clarified, standardized, and adopted by others. Instead, he is transcribing the intellectual atmosphere in which his critical operations are situated. Since experience may be shared or attained, since talent is not infrequently bestowed or developed, what factor distinguishes between the circle of understanding as it is described and as it is practiced by Spitzer? Faith. "For every poem the critic needs a separate inspiration, a separate light from above (it is this constant need which makes for humility, and it is the accumulation of past enlightenments that encourages a sort of pious confidence). Indeed, a Protean mutability is required of the critic, for the device which has proved successful for one work of art cannot be applied mechanically to another" (Spitzer, *Linguistics and Literary History*, p. 28). Thus, it is faith—in the intrinsic unity within each artistic form, in the "light from above" which provides the key enabling us to penetrate that unity—which characterizes Spitzer's utilization and understanding of the philological circle. For Spitzer, each critical act mandates a separate appeal to the heavens; one must be in a state of grace in order to initiate such an appeal, so one undergoes a purification ritual by ordering one's life and making choices of a moral nature.

That art is present in every act of literary explication most of us would not dispute. Spitzer moves beyond this to assert that in the beginning there was God and the mystery of his ways. Each critical act of elucidation allows us to perceive a sense of the nature of God: "That an etymology can be found by man is a miracle. An etymology introduces meaning into the meaningless." Indeed, Spitzer believes that the entire discipline of philology is distinguished by precisely this human awareness of what is immortal. It is "the preestablished firm conviction, the 'axion,' of the philologian [rather than 'philologist'—to echo 'theologian'], that details are not an inchoate chance aggregation of dispersed material through which no light shines. The philologian must believe in the existence of some light from on high" (Spitzer, *Linguistics and Literary History*, pp. 6, 54).

On a personal level, however, a successful critical act signifies a small approval by God of his particular literary agent. That is why humility is necessary before looking to God for the inspiration that provides the click which initiates the circle. That is why Spitzer cannot predict when he or anyone else will experience the click: how could he presume to order that which he believes to be the province of God? "It is the accumulation of past enlightenments that encourages a sort of pious confidence": pious, certainly, for the entire endeavor would not be possible without the light from above, and confidence would accurately describe the quality of assuredness in the practice of the philological circle after repeated successes with the method. But to refer to several acts of accomplished literary interpretation as "the accumulation of past enlightenments" reveals to us Spitzer's conception of the click and the exegesis that follows it. Whoever practices the method of the philological circle—from the click of inspiration to the penetration of the inner unity—realizes that the truth which he has come to understand about the inner form of artistic expression is itself a part of a larger truth and an encompassing form—that which is dictated from on high to us all. It can be seen, I think, that for Spitzer a career composed of isolated essays devoted to literary explication will, to say the least, present a portrait of a man on whom Providence has smiled by its continuous bestowal of sublime inspiration in the service of its truth.

An attitude of spiritual enlightenment is usually accompanied by a moral imperative to communicate the revealed truth to others. The public, then, not only influences the literary critic as he conceives of the text he will analyze and the text he will write; it is itself influenced by the critic's enlightened vision of truth about literary history—a knowledge that is "the best document of a nation." This awareness of Spitzer's perceived obligation to spread his far-reaching enlightened insights over an extended general public provides us with another perspective on the frequent criticism that Spitzer is excessively combative and pugnacious in his work.

Wellek noted that Spitzer is often "criticized for his indulgence in fierce polemics, but one should recognize that they are part of his process of self-definition."[11] Quite a pertinent idea, although the question of why he sought to define himself in such a fashion is still more fundamental:

I have often been asked why I devote so much of my efforts to "destructive criticism." The answer is that I believe that, in the discipline of Philology as in the sciences, the ultimate goal, however more arduous its attainment or approximation, must be Truth and that the failure to expose contentment with half-truths or non-truths would amount to a conspiracy of silence against that noble discipline. [12]

Spitzer's dedication to "the ultimate goal" of "Truth" and his determination that truth is to be found in the click which descends from above demonstrates that, for him, each article, each insight, is significant and important, for every benign turn of the philological circle serves to expose and weaken the position of those determinists for whom divine intuition is, at best, a shoddy intellectual practice. Further, since what we know about literature opens new vistas into our awareness of history and culture, a series of isolated truths (Spitzer's articles), produced in a coherent discipline (philology), provides a unified and enduring truth about our lives, our history, and our world: "details are not an inchoate chance aggregation of dispersed material through which no light shines." For Spitzer, then, his collection of articles about a wide variety of literary subjects formulates, when taken together, at least one persistent refrain: the attainable possibilities for individual and world harmony that ensue once one is attuned to an awareness of Spirit.

The quest for truth in language and literature on a national level is what motivates Spitzer to attempt to discern "the innermost strivings of the nation." Since he believed that "the idea *and* the word are, at every moment of the reading, *seen* together," his words on literature—which he conceived and created in the United States— are necessarily unified with his ideas on literature. Because of the unity of idea and word, the writing of literary criticism in the United States carries with it the moral duty to rise to the truth about such criticism and its country of origin. "Thus the individual human soul, though a minimal thing in this infinite space, can attune itself to the whole world."[13]

It is the Spirit from on high that regulates our intellectual perceptions according to "a law of continuous metamorphosis": "nothing stands alone, individual, and separate; everything is fitted into the Whole—in fact, represents the Whole; no *one* aspect is ever valid."[14] In the midst of the flux of historical life, the contemplation of literature allows us to commune with all that is timeless and eternal: "The greatest works of art have, indeed, the power, after making us see the most unexpected perspectives, of restoring, to the renewed world, that primeval simplicity and richness which it must have had on the first day of creation, that inner beatitude of self-enjoying beauty that is as well God-like as child-like."[15]

If the greatest works of literary art possess—through their unique vantage point—the power to return us to a sense of the original purity and serenity that existed on the newly created earth; if, as well, literary art provides us with the best method of understanding a nation; if the language and literature of that nation can be explicated profoundly by an enlightened mind infused with an inspirational quality of spirit; and finally, if the explicator interacts with and is influenced by the public of that nation and its innermost strivings,

93

then we are faced with a human history which is simultaneously a history of spirit and essence; a history in time which concerns itself with tracing the persistent glimpses of the timeless through time; a history of mind and order which is to be delineated through intuition and randomness. "Obviously, life asks for a harmony between words and deeds."[16] Thus, in accordance with his own conception of the world, Spitzer posits the need for a reconciliation between literature and history, fantasy and fact, language and society, our world of illusion and world without end. To help initiate such an enormous undertaking, to begin "taming the monster by style," to "fight [his] way to [the] unity,"[17] he sees one man equipped with the requisite talent, experience, and faith. That man is Leo Spitzer.

In order to accommodate this impression of Spitzer's accomplishment with earlier observations about his work, it is necessary to take Spitzer at his word and examine portions of his work to uncover and disclose his "constancy and unity of approach." Traditionally, critics have assumed that Spitzer's mental acquisitiveness was limited to obtaining a strong, scholarly command of those isolated texts with which he dealt, and fell short of any consistent thematic or philosophical enunciation. Rather than approaching Spitzer as a profound source of scholarly expertise on a vast range of literary and philological topics (on this level, his article-by-article contribution prevails, spanning languages, disciplines, literary genres and periods), I propose to read him in order to discern those *"leitmotifs or refrains"* which Spitzer felt constituted the inner unity of his life's work and which reflected the soul of his authorial identity. Such a pursuit requires that we formulate a context by which we, as Americans, can evaluate Leo Spitzer's American work. In so doing, we shall be exploring the lines of demarcation between literary criticism and history which currently exist and which underscored Spitzer's work. Thus, in some measure, we shall be establishing ourselves as the public with which Spitzer, the author, critic, and historian, meant to interact.

Leo Spitzer was born on February 7, 1887, in Vienna, Austria—

the fin-de-siècle Vienna of Freud, Schnitzler, Robert Musil, Wittgenstein, and Arnold Schoenberg. Spitzer felt that many aspects of Viennese culture and thought exerted a significant influence on his intellectual development. For instance, he credits his decision to study Romance languages in general, and French in particular, as stemming from

> my native Vienna, the gay and orderly, skeptic and sentimental, Catholic and pagan Vienna of yore, . . . filled with adoration of the French way of life. I had always been surrounded by a French atmosphere and, at that juvenile stage of experience, had acquired a picture, perhaps overgeneralized, of French literature, which seemed to me definable by an Austrian-like mixture of sensuousness and reflection, of vitality and discipline, of sentimentality and critical wit. [18]

"Atmosphere," according to Spitzer, helped shape men's thought and ideas. Accordingly, let us examine a few descriptions of the intellectual atmosphere of the Vienna of Spitzer's youth to conceive his intellectual development.

"Vienna in the *fin de siècle*, with its acutely felt tremors of social and political disintegration, proved one of the most fertile breeding grounds of our century's a-historical culture. Its great intellectual innovators . . . all broke, more or less deliberately, their ties to the historical outlook central to the nineteenth century liberal culture in which they had been reared." So writes Carl E. Schorske in his *Fin-De-Siècle Vienna*.[19] Displayed beside this is Spitzer's frequent warning "to all cultural theorizers against building their fallacious architectures on the quicksand of the transient state of their own historical information rather than on abiding facts of culture."[20] Spitzer's inclination to expand traditional historical rubrics in order to include spiritual, cultural, and stylistic-impressionistic criteria may thus be rooted in his Viennese experience. "The idea of regarding language, symbolisms and media of expression of all kinds as giving us 'representations' (*Darstellungen*) or 'pictures' (*Bilder*) had by 1910 become a commonplace in all fields of Viennese cultural debate," according to Allan Janik and Stephen Toulmin in their *Wittgenstein's Vienna*.[21] In this might be found one basis for Spitzer's belief that the manifestations of language represent an author's interior truth, and that the conceptualization of literary art presents a picture of the inner soul of its nation.

Spitzer's father was an affluent Jewish merchant who was ambivalent about his identity as a businessman; he emphasized a professional career for his son. Although the Spitzer family was assimilated into the customary flow of Viennese life, Judaism was yet a powerful influence on them:

My father was not particularly pious. He was a liberal, care-free, jovial Viennese, but he never thought of deserting his faith. We fasted on the Day of Atonement, and on the high holidays we went to the synagogue together.

For a few years I was deeply impressed with the religious ceremonies of the synagogue and I wanted to become a rabbi. But when I learned more of classical antiquity, I found that Horace and Sophocles spoke more to my heart than did the Psalter and the Prophets. Later Ronsard and Racine, Dante and Calderón came into my life.

But the profound imprint of Judaism remained. It is monotheistic; like the giants Freud and Einstein, I found my thinking influenced toward the tracing of things to a single origin.[22]

That Spitzer would speak of his work as "the tracing of things to a single origin"; that he would attribute this to the influence of Judaism and its monotheistic emphasis; that he would equate religious texts with literary ones (and suggest the equation of religious ritual with linguistic structure): all of this serves to reinforce our contention that Spitzer believed his historical literary methods were derived from (and integrally related to) an ahistorical religious truth. Further, his association of himself with Freud and Einstein suggests that he viewed himself as exemplary, as possessing the optimal blend of experience, talent, and faith necessary for the attainment of philological spirit. Spitzer's habit of including personal and autobiographical details in the body of his literary critical texts attests to his confidence that the life and experience of the intuitionist are inseparable from the intuited insights which form the basis for the article. Such confidence is often rooted in the self-reliance that stems from a comfortable childhood.

This precocious poise was evident when Spitzer, as a young child, lost his mother: "My (Jewish) father used to require tears from me when we would visit the grave of my mother, whom I had lost at an early age, as if the actual shedding of tears were a guarantee of the feeling which should elicit them. But I distinctly remember that I felt unable to weep because of an inner opposition against a set form."[23] This anecdote, included in an article on patterns of etymology and thought, is then used by Spitzer to compare his attitude as a young child to the stance of young civilizations in general and the Protestant religion in particular: that they are "suspicious of forms" in comparison to the more primal belief of the "earliest pagan, Jewish, Mohammedan, and Catholic civilizations." It should not be difficult to observe that Spitzer developed an unusual mode of thought which, in every instance, equates his personal inner experience with the deep truth of historical and cultural reality.

In 1905, Spitzer was graduated at the head of his class from Franz-Joseph Gymnasium in Vienna with a bachelor of arts degree. While attending school, he had become infused with the ideal of a scholarly life devoted to literature: "My generation in a gymnasium of Vienna was educated, not so much by our teachers, however excellent they may have been, but directly by Socrates or Goethe, before whom they effaced themselves. The life of a Socrates or a Goethe was presented to us as the noblest that man could live, a life of spiritual pursuits rather than of material welfare or technical accomplishment."[24] Again, that this statement was included in an article on the formation of the American humanist emphasizes Spitzer's avowal that his development as *an* American humanist is equivalent to the envisioning of a humanist in ideal form.

Spitzer enrolled at the University of Vienna, where he studied with the Swiss Romance philologist Wilhelm Meyer-Lübke. During his first year, attending lectures with hundreds of other students, listening to Meyer-Lübke speak on seemingly obscure points of French historical grammar, Spitzer was "at the brink of total desperation," for while much was said about the derivation of specific sounds and letters in the French language, nothing was mentioned of the French people and culture in which the language flourished.[25] Spitzer weathered his bout with intellectual confusion and despair; he continued his course of study that would provide him with a unique background for his literary and historical work: "It was the benignity of Providence, exploiting my native Teutonic docility toward scholars who knew more than I, which kept me faithful to the study of Romance philology. By not abandoning prematurely this sham science, by seeking, instead, to appropriate it, I came to recognize its true value as well as my own possibilities of work—and to establish my life's goal."[26] Here, Spitzer received an early and fundamental indication that a mass of supposedly chaotic and isolated facts might be unified by an inner cohesion. His crediting of Providence for the ordering of his educational life reveals the extent to which he identifies the spirit which regulated his destiny with the spirit which guided the path of history and language. And the fact that Spitzer, who had earlier been unable to weep at his mother's death due to his resistance to the "set form" of mourning, had been so upset and then found clarity, supports a possible revelatory interpretation for his designated career.

Armed with a sense of purpose, Spitzer continued his studies, often under difficult conditions: "During my years of study I saw Meyer-Lübke only in lecture rooms and seminars, with the exception of two private conferences, the one lasting five minutes when I was choosing my thesis, the other, lasting two minutes, when I learned about the acceptance of this thesis."[27] Spitzer's dissertation was completed in 1910;[28] in it, he "dealt with Rabelais' comic word-formations, a subject to which I was attracted because of certain affinities between Rabelaisian and Viennese (Nestroy!) comic writing, and which offered the opportunity of bridging the gap between linguistic and literary history."[29] In attaining the Ph.D. degree, and in presenting a thesis that attempted to transcend previously accepted boundaries between linguistic and literary history, Spitzer took the first steps toward rising to his "vision of scholarship."[30] He believed that the path to intellectual clarity and knowledge ran parallel with the path to religious grace and serenity: "Love, whether it be love for God, love for one's fellow men, or the love of art, can only gain by the effort of the human intellect to search for the reasons of its most sublime emotions, and to formulate them."[31]

Following the traditional example of self-assured children from wealthy families who are certain that they will ultimately receive an inheritance, Spitzer continued his studies beyond the doctoral level, delighting in the opportunity to obtain learning for its own sake: "I had no thought of professional scholarly work. I would be an amateur. I would do nice things, read and write on philology, but I would do nothing in the way of a career." Spitzer devoted a year to studies in Paris, a semester to studies in Leipzig, and a semester to studies in Rome. As a youth in Vienna, Spitzer learned French, German, Hebrew, and Hungarian; as a result of his graduate and postdoctoral education, Spitzer added Latin, Greek, English, Italian, Provençal, Spanish, Portuguese, Catalan, Rumanian, Gothic, Anglo-Saxon, Sanskrit, Lithuanian, Old Church Slavonic, Albanian, and Neo-Greek.[32] It was in Leipzig that Spitzer studied with the French literary historian, Philipp August Becker. Although Spitzer was a more mature scholar than the first-year student who listened to Meyer-Lübke, he experienced a similar perplexity: Becker seemed to dwell upon a curiously abstract literary history that did not follow from the examined texts: "Not only was this kind of humanities not centered on a particular people in a particular time, but the subject matter itself had got lost: Man."[33]

At this point in his intellectual development, Spitzer was attempting to build upon the methods of Meyer-Lübke and Becker in order to devise a personal procedure that would enable him to study man as the subject matter. The questions he wished to address to literary works were not conceivable within the analytical systems of his teachers: "what made them works of art, what was expressed in them, and why these expressions appeared . . . at that particular time."[34] Since these principles constitute a historical relativistic formulation, and since we have already seen that Spitzer was dubious about historical relativism as a method or world view, it should be possible to rework these considerations in line with what we accept as Spitzer's concerns. Therefore, Spitzer was interested in the spiritual (or timeless) history of man across time.

Upon his return to Vienna in 1913, Meyer-Lübke invited Spitzer to serve as a *Privatdozent* at the University of Vienna. It was a fortunate position for a young scholar. Under the modest support of the university, and with a light teaching load, he would devote his full time to scholarly research and await his eventual calling to a professorship. For Spitzer, this appointment seemed ideal. As an heir apparent, practical financial considerations were not important to him, but he viewed the opportunity to enter the academy as a rare and prestigious one: "It was an unforgettable moment of my life when I was given access for the first time to the faculty room of the University of Vienna where I saw the over-life-sized marble statues of Sophocles and Hippocrates quietly exhorting me to lead a life similar to theirs."[35]

Undoubtedly, Spitzer would have relished a long tenure as the university-supported humanities scholar. But the outbreak of the First World War in 1914 interrupted his budding career: Spitzer was drafted into the Austrian army. He had the "good fortune" to be assigned to the bureau of censorship, where he directed the Italian department. All correspondence relating to Italian prisoners of war was routed to Spitzer's section in Vienna. What aroused his interest was the manner in which the hungry prisoners of war, in an attempt to alert their relatives to their plight and receive food and provisions through the mail, resorted to various circumlocutory expressions to indicate their hunger and pass the perusal of the censors. A simple understatement in periphrastic form would have been sufficient to alert the family and escape the censor's wrath. But Spitzer found that the more imaginative and creative soldiers devised elaborate fictional and poetic conceits in which to conceal their messages. These obtrusive literary lapses in the epistolary form achieved the opposite of their intended effect: the censors were alerted.

In the midst of a war, and despite the distasteful task of weeding out appeals for more food in order to ensure hunger, Spitzer was heartened and delighted by his interpretation of the soldiers' letters. Even during times of hardship and deprivation, men were attracted by the lofty appeals of art, supplanting the mundane signals of hunger. According to Spitzer, the urge to be creative and original overcame the original desire to launch a stealthy appeal past the censor. Thus, a harmony existed that united mankind in the contemplation of art and transcended national barriers. In effect, Spitzer's identification of himself as a humanist and a Romance philologist was so profound that it remained with him throughout his military service: he functioned in the bureau of censorship as a linguist in the service of art and Spirit. At the war's end, he would write a book about the imaginative compositions of the hungry Italian soldiers.[36]

That Spitzer was able to read the letters as literary texts and interpret the circumlocutory passages as expressions of the soldiers' psychological state attests to the influence on Spitzer of his fellow Viennese citizen Sigmund Freud. A psychoanalytical explanation of the literary tendency among the prisoners might suggest that the creative impetus served as a defense mechanism by which the debilitating sensation of extreme hunger and its accompanying psychological deprivation could possibly be diminished; the imaginative flights would help transcend the bleak reality of the soldiers. Spitzer's perception of Freud's theories allowed him to detect the phenomenon in the letters originally. But his interpretation of his war experience took a different direction:

And the letters proved to be fascinatingly interesting from the point of view of linguistics.

101

These Italian soldiers were simple people, yet they had astounding literary talent. Among all the correspondence I saw, the Italian letters were the most naturally artistic. This was the first time that the inner life of a whole nation had been displayed before me. It was wonderful! The letters were filled with love and, unfortunately, hunger, but love and hunger turned simple country boys into universal poets. [37]

The literary letters were not a testimony of the behavior and talents of a particular people at a particular time under special circumstances; rather, they provided evidence, for Spitzer, of the "naturally artistic" literary talent of the Italian soldiers. The prisoners were not to be thought of primarily as talented individuals; instead, their letters signified the "inner life" of the Italian nation.

Does it necessarily follow, however, that because a group of Italian prisoners of war developed a literary tendency that ran counter to their intended purpose of surreptitiously obtaining food the entire Italian nation is blessed with this artistic talent? Spitzer would hold that it does, for the organism—in this case, "the inner life of a whole nation"—is "everywhere the same." The literary letters were only one means of tapping down to the core of inner truth. It was for this reason that Spitzer looked upon his assignment to the bureau of censorship as being good fortune: for had he not been so positioned, he would never have been able to intuit the inner truth about Italy. Similarly, although it was unfortunate that the soldiers had to endure severe hunger, their condition prompted their artistic expression which, through the vehicle of Spitzer's book of the letters, was revealed to the world as universal poetry. The sanctity of one's personal perceptions is surely a matter of faith; but with that assuredness, vast intellectual structures may be built upon those individual sense impressions.

The end of the war brought many changes to the Austrian nation and to Leo Spitzer. In 1918, he accepted an appointment at the University of Bonn on a meager stipend. Financial considerations were of no serious concern, however, for Spitzer's father had died, leaving Leo a millionaire. During the early twenties, Spitzer married and sired a child while writing and teaching at Bonn. But the rampant inflation that decimated Germany and Austria during those years leading up to the great inflation of 1923 devoured Spitzer's fortune, leaving him entirely dependent upon his university earnings. Providence provides, and then it takes away. What was Spitzer's response? "It had looked as though I were cut out to be a noble parasite. It turned out I was just a worker. This was the better thing" (Spitzer, "Interview," p. 21). For many persons, a devastating change of circumstances and identity experienced during one's mid-thirties would provoke confusion, disorientation, even depression; for Spitzer to claim serene acceptance as his response to these events indicates that his principal identification dealt with philology and with his faith in the Providence which regulated it, and him, and all of us.

It seems evident that, during the years of Spitzer's early university appointments, a belief in an overall constancy composed of small changes characterized his life and work. In 1925, Spitzer accepted his first full professorship at the University of Marburg, where he spent five happy years: an atmosphere of harmony accompanied the ordinary daily contact between the faculty and the students ("And amid the simple gaiety, serious study thrived"). But in 1930, lured by the attractiveness of "an amazingly high salary," Spitzer moved to the University of Cologne, where he was not so content: "No true scholarship could be accomplished in the atmosphere of Cologne. Life was too satisfactory. Many professors were interested only in the cars and wine that their new prosperity could buy" (Spitzer, "Interview," p. 21). It was as if his colleagues had accepted the financial inducement (and, perhaps, Spitzer himself), and made the wrong moral choices, and, thus, were unable to delve successfully into the scholarly truth.

But other moral choices of a dubious nature were being made in Germany at this time. In 1933, the University of Cologne received a telegram from the minister of public education: in accordance with

Hitler's policy, Spitzer, as a Jew, was ordered to "take a leave of absence." Since tenured professors had been dismissed only under the rarest of circumstances, Spitzer realized the severity of the national situation: "I decided to leave the country immediately." Although he was offered a position by the University of Manchester, and although he was able to brush up on his English to an acceptable capacity, Spitzer declined the job because the courses he was expected to teach were too basic. At a time of danger, Spitzer—"with brazen confidence"—decided to wait for a better job offer (Spitzer, "Interview," p. 26).

Such confidence was highly unusual at a time when many people lacked the financial means and the overseas opportunity requisite for flight from Germany. Spitzer, having both, and feeling with certainty that his future was in peril, concluded that he could do better. On what basis did he come to his decision? Certainly not by a political or a historical means of analysis, for according to those standards, his decision appears problematic. Such a decision did, however, demonstrate his dedication to philology and his insistence upon the proper educational standards for its transmittal; further, it subjugated himself, and his family, to the will of divine Providence in a manner suggesting the proper mode for a moral critic to approach a text passively, according to Spitzer's method. Spitzer's choice might be viewed as an attempt to return to pure scholarship. Such a return to the spiritual scholarship touted by Spitzer mandated sacrifice and an appropriate serene acceptance of the stipulations of the divinity. All of this Spitzer was willing to experience—and perhaps for that reason, he soon received word of another university position.

As Germany was engaged in weeding out supposedly undesirable members of its universities, Turkey was in the process of developing its educational system. Many professors who had lost their positions in Germany and Austria were invited to teach at the University of Istanbul, and Spitzer was among them. In late 1933, Spitzer journeyed to Istanbul with his family. His position involved serving as an administrator as well as an educator: as the lone philologist, he was in charge of coordinating classes in four languages for several thousand students. In addition, he lectured to his classes—through an interpreter—in French and used a multitude of other languages to communicate with his teaching staff. The problem with this new appointment was that "there were almost no books"; the dean's reply to Spitzer's query was that books were not significant since they were so easily combustible (Spitzer, "Interview," p. 26).

Might Spitzer have been better off accepting the University of Manchester offer? Could "true scholarship" as Spitzer envisioned it occur at the University of Istanbul without books? It is clear that Spitzer did not think along these lines. In part, he was able to obtain sustenance from the ample personal library that he was able to transport to Turkey. More essentially, however, he viewed himself as fitting the contours of a vast and harmonious world plan—one in which he, as a man with experience, talent, and faith, could provide a significant contribution through perception: "For a harmonious and poised man is apt, by nature, to see everywhere himself, and the things connected with himself, as being 'embraced' and caressed: to feel that he is the center of a whole—the embryo in the egg, the tree within its bark, the earth wrapped round by ether. This is an inner form, a living pattern of thought, which must reproduce itself unceasingly."[38] Thus, Spitzer—in Istanbul—concentrated upon "the inner form": with the "brazen confidence" that comes from placing one's faith in Providence, he viewed his surroundings—despite their shortcomings—as being vitalized by a divine spirit. Years later, in an essay on Paul Claudel, Spitzer notes that "Claudel sees the cities framed by Nature: in his vision the two are not opposed to each other, but are fused—a fusion which is so characteristic of our modern landscape." He supports Claudel's perception by his own anecdotal recollection: "I think I shall never forget the impression made on me by the noisy streets of Istanbul teeming with gesticulating and screaming Southerners and the solemn quiet of the Bosporus and the mountains of Asia—boundless beyond man's gaze."[39] And then the matter is dispensed with. It is as if Spitzer, finding that his own experience bears out Claudel's insight, has no need for further discussion of the issue: he and Claudel are in harmony; the inner form has been attained. In another essay on why languages change, Spitzer refers to his memory of the way newsboys in Istanbul called out for the evening paper—thus, years later, every experience is connected with the "harmonious and poised man," and he "see[s] everywhere himself."[40]

Yet all was not so pristine: Europe was preparing for a massive conflagration; the quality of the world's moral choices seemed to indicate a state of spiritual disharmony; the likelihood of serious study—in an upwardly mobile but resource-deficient institution—appeared bleak. After one year at Istanbul, Spitzer was offered a position at the Johns Hopkins University in Baltimore. Having experienced the burdens of administrative responsibility, the prospect of a job that required only teaching and research seemed delightful. But he was bound to honor his three-year contract; would Johns Hopkins hold his position for two more years?

From Spitzer's point of view, how could it be otherwise? Hopkins agreed to wait for him, and in 1936, Spitzer and his family emigrated to the United States. As usual, in retrospect, Spitzer held that events had proceeded for the best: "In Istanbul I could play Caesar, but I was Caesar to a village."[41] At key junctures in Spitzer's life, when he was in need of aid or comfort or fortuitous circumstances, he placed himself at the disposal of God, and as we have seen, he was not disappointed about any crucial concern. What literary method could possibly be more appropriate to such a man and his life—be more true to his inner form—than the philological circle, whereby one places oneself at the disposal of Providence in order to await the revelatory click of insight! As a result of his movements from Europe to Turkey to the United States, Spitzer "relived" what he would later describe as "the basic Jewish experience": "the contrast between a life in the center which is peace and equilibrium and a life in the corner which is restless striving toward the center."[42] And it is this experience—to strive from a corner bastion toward a center of peace and harmony—that will characterize Spitzer's work in the United States.

At the Johns Hopkins University, where he became an American citizen, Spitzer was, at first, "isolated and had only a few devoted students."[43] But such a situation only intensified his efforts to arrive at the truth about the inner essence of the American public and the American nation. He wished to obtain a knowledge of "not only the intricacies of English syntax and stylistics, but some of the more recondite features of American culture and of its particular moral, logical, and aesthetic aspirations: a knowledge without which all endeavors of the philologist to explain poetry to an American public must fail completely."[44] In this task, he was aided by his student, protégée, and Hopkins colleague, Anna Granville Hatcher, toward whom Spitzer always expressed gratitude and professional affection.[45] Spitzer's challenge was to live as an American while attempting to "read" the United States as a text. Thus, he was required to stand outside of what he was attempting to become one with. Part of the difficulty, he felt, was that "the American way of life seems to admit no relativism, linguistic or otherwise." He does not mean the historical relativism which, as we have seen, Spitzer believes objectifies the necessary moral ramifications of literature. Rather, he refers to the relativism that allows a person to differentiate between the body which experiences and the mind which analyzes that experience. According to Spitzer, a humanist is "devoted to man and to an understanding of man. The humanist should live among his fellow-men. He should not lose contact with them, for then he would be no longer humane himself; but he should live somewhat removed from them."[46] An emissary of truth and Western civilization living and working in the New World, but whose intellectual roots and habitual state of mind emanate from an Old World identification: it is not difficult to visualize what Spitzer's self-conception must have been.

As the world steeled itself for war, Spitzer envisioned that at least one precipitate factor was a change in Western civilization: "the increasing loss of inner life—a characteristic, influenced by many historical factors, of our civilization that tends toward the encouragement of the 'chauffeur mentality.' "[47] In order to penetrate to the truth about a nation's inner life, there must first exist an inner life capable of being explicated. In the United States, Spitzer again felt himself manipulated by Providence to be the right person in the right time under the right circumstances in the right place: only he—with his profound faith and vitality of Spirit—could best act to renew the United States' continuity with the Spirit inherent in the Western humanistic tradition. The inspiration and clarity of his faith enabled Spitzer to believe that his historical background and experience, and his personal talents, could best be utilized to rekindle the United States' inner spirit as he came to know it—to unify a commitment to Spirit with the creation of Spirit through language. The purpose would be, borrowing Spitzer's description of Shakespeare and Milton, to lift us "as is done by sublime music, from the oppression of time into timelessness, from the burden of sin toward communion with God; and our battle with time (once we lost paradise, once again we shall regain it) results in everlasting triumph."[48]

As a sophisticated European cosmopolitan transplanted to Baltimore, Spitzer's conceptualization of his task echoed the words of another Viennese artist who emigrated to the United States, Arnold Schoenberg: "Alas, it is one thing to envision in a creative instant of inspiration and it is another thing to materialize one's vision by painstakingly connecting details until they fuse into a kind of organism."[49] Hence, Spitzer realized that the profession of humanistic faith, in order to be effective, must not be perceived as a harangue. The endless holding forth on one theme, although consistent, would impress the public as being tedious and boring. But how to isolate the particular occasions that would initiate literary and critical treatment? Spitzer's solution was in perfect accord with his critical method: he would read the United States as a text, subjugate himself to its various nuances and intricacies, and await the click of inspiration that would dictate his subject and procedure. The fact that the searching of the United States for substance and material was identical to the process of being alive in the United States would not be perceived by Spitzer as incongruous; on the contrary, he embraces the manifestation of the harmony between the mundane and the sublime: *"Methode ist Erlebnis* [method is experience], Gundolf has said."[50] And in this, too, it is possible to detect a similarity with Schoenberg: "In fact, the concept of creator and creation should be formed in harmony with the Divine Model; inspiration and perfection, wish and fulfillment, will and accomplishment coincide spontaneously and simultaneously"—and with his Germanic intellectual heritage.[51]

Spitzer found one of his first American subjects at his own university in the work of his Hopkins colleague Arthur Lovejoy.[52] Spitzer viewed Lovejoy's formulation of the history of ideas as a barren and reductive conception to be distinguished from the European *Geistesgeschichte,* which Spitzer found to be more "synthetic" and holistic, and toward which he felt more sympathetic.[53] While the European mode of analysis implemented a unified notion of Spirit upon which the subsequent treatment of literature rested, Spitzer felt that the history of ideas forcibly wrested ideas from their literary context, thus distorting them and rendering them next to useless as a means to comprehend literature and the world that engages it. Since he believed that "so often it is true that language reveals and even modifies general tendencies of thought or feelings," it was inappropriate to isolate ideas from the language that creates them, and he perceived Lovejoy's discipline as perpetuating that trend.[54]

In his essay "History of Ideas Versus Reading of Poetry" (1941), Spitzer attempted to expose the shortcomings of Lovejoy's method; in so doing, he was able to clarify his own thoughts in relation to his identity as an American scholar: "My main objection against this untimely procedure lies in the belief that one must first *see* a phenomenon as a unit, before one can rightfully inquire into its history. . . . The history of a thing can be established only when it exists—exists, at least, in the mind of the historian; otherwise the history in question has no 'hero,' no subject."[55] An entity must be "seen"—perceived—as a totality before any investigation of its history is launched. But how may one perceive a phenomenon as a whole without knowing something of its history? Through the intuited click of a spiritual cognition: an impulsive creation of the entire unit based upon a devout contemplation of its surface existence. Through his faith in the Providence which oversees the use of the philological circle, and his stipulation that the contemplated phenomenon is everywhere the same, Spitzer suggests that cognitive structure precedes essence. Only when the historian has a vision of his subject matter preexistent in his mind can he begin to investigate the nature of that subject matter. To a certain extent, this is a valid concept, for when one initiates a historical inquiry, one must possess an affiliative sense of the contours of that exploration. But Spitzer is here proposing that history begins with the enlightened inner vision of an inspired perceiver.

Thus, "art and *outward reality* should, at least while the work of art is being studied, be kept separate": it is the revelatory click of inner awareness that provides us with the nature of an entity as a unit; yet it is from this inward reality of art that we obtain the insight by which we conceive of knowledge about our outward reality—our nation, our history, our civilization. Is Spitzer here anticipating the position of many contemporary critics who hold that there is no truth to be obtained, only the subjective perspective of the individual author? Since he believed—as I indicated earlier—that "the ultimate goal . . . must be Truth," it is clear that he is not. Preferable to the history of ideas would be "a poised and self-contained aesthetic meditation before a particular work of art that is unique and unrepeatable by its nature." With the poise derived from faith in Spirit, the unique individual cogitates upon a unique work of art and thus obtains an awareness of our collective, general truth. In this way, history exists first in the mind of the historian, or rather, exists for that historian who embraces the mystical relationship between inner vision and outer manifestation: "precisely because the work of art is 'as much in him as in itself,' there is no necessity, as far as the aesthetic response is concerned, for the reader to be made historical minded."[56]

It does not follow, however, that because Spitzer opposed the grafting of supposedly extraneous historical facts upon the pure function of literary interpretation, he did not support a conceptualization of history or emphasize the relationship between history and philology. Indeed, in *"Geistesgeschichte* vs. History of Ideas as Applied to Hitlerism" (1944)—another article drafted in response to an original essay by Arthur Lovejoy—Spitzer attempts to clarify his notion of history-touched-by-spirit. In the midst of the Second World War, Lovejoy proposes that one means of understanding Hitlerism would be to explore the history of German thought; from out of the German Romantic period he isolates several ideas which, he holds, have evolved into the Hitlerism of the moment. Thus, history is cohesive, and we can envision the present as growing out of the past. Spitzer not only disapproves of this on an intellectual level, he resists such a theory on a personal basis as well, for it suggests that Spitzer's own intellectual roots may be perceived as antecedents to Hitlerism. The European-nurtured Spirit that Spitzer wishes to expound, and which he hopes will thrive, must not be presented to the American public as violent and totalitarian!

In response to an article written in history about a historical reality, Spitzer produces his conception of a sacrosanct history immune from the vulgar alterations of time. Since Lovejoy isolates ideas from their historical context, Spitzer insists that "it is a bias to believe that understanding must always wait on definition." Instead, Spitzer emphasizes direct, holistic vision: an idea is not "detachable from the soul of the man who begot or received the idea, from the spiritual climate which nourished it." Here, Spitzer underlines the idea that history emanates from the souls of men; these inner-driven men—when considered together—form the spiritual climate from which we receive historical actions and thoughts. The structure of our outward reality, then, is shaped in accordance with an inward formulation—

and such an inner motivation presupposes a commitment to (or a passionate allegiance to) the divine Spirit that regulates souls: "important ideas are from the start a *passionate* response to problems which agitate their period."[57] Historical ideas cannot be detached from the passionate humans who devised them or the turbulent circumstances that motivated their creation: historical ideas must be seen as providing evidence of the spiritual process in man across time.

If the romantic period was so influential in the fomentation of the Hitleristic philosophy, Spitzer questions "why the period immediately following upon Romanticism was attended with such a marvelous expansion in all fields of the humanities. It was then that modern philology, linguistics, history of art, folklore, etc., were brought to birth." And, of course, Spitzer's world view and philological circle developed from out of that intellectual climate. For Spitzer, his own orientation is not to be perceived as an aberration in the evolution of German fascism: Hitlerism represents the deviation from the right, and any method (such as Lovejoy's) that associates a perverse tendency (nazism) with an intellectual mainstream (romanticism) has not benefited from the divine-inspired click which accompanies the circle of understanding. Hence, Lovejoy's hypothesis—that the influence of romantic ideas on the "educated and reading public" resulted in the appearance of Hitlerism—inspires Spitzer to respond: "Indeed, it was the humanistic spirit of the classics and of Kant which managed to counterbalance the strong nationalistic tendencies which betrayed themselves in the *Gymnasien* . . . it was precisely *not* the educated and reading public which had become conditioned for Nazism: it was from quite other ranks of society that Hitler recruited his followers" (Spitzer, "*Geistesgeschichte* vs. History of Ideas," pp. 196, 200). An effete and dastardly philosophy could not possibly proceed from out of a literate, humanistic public, for it is the educated populace of the nation that influences— and is influenced by—those literary works which possess the imprint of the spiritual essence of a higher harmony: it is impossible for

Lovejoy to be in possession of "the true analysis." Hitlerism did not advance within that bastion of humanistic strength, the educated public "who formed the backbone of German culture," but, rather, within "the masses of the uneducated" who had multiplied as a result of social conditions. Once Lovejoy's historical evidence is shown to be flawed, so, too, must be his conclusion: "Thus there is no continuity of teaching from the Schlegels to Hitler; between them there is a cultural break caused by social upheaval" (Spitzer, "*Geistesgeschichte* vs. History of Ideas," pp. 200, 201).

It is evident that Spitzer conceives of the necessity to discredit Lovejoy in the largest possible terms: the educated American public, heir to the spiritual greatness of the American nation, must not be deprived of the realization that they are in harmony with the humanistic tradition of Germany and Austria—in effect, during a time of war and discord, all men need to embrace the truth that they are, fundamentally and intrinsically, united and at peace. That Spitzer's words are intense and emotional is without question. But it is intriguing that he did not construct his impassioned defense of humanism in response to the outward reality of his times; instead, he was inspired to action by a specific article about a literary period and the consequences of that period. Spitzer did not feel motivated to directly refute Hitler and his ideology (as Auerbach was impelled); he was aroused to confront Hitler indirectly as a result of his perception of Lovejoy's article. This is because he believed that "it is not the letter of any idea, or any set of ideas, but the 'spirit' in which the ideas are carried out and allowed to associate with each other—it is the total system of ideas charged with emotion that explains an historical movement" (Spitzer, "*Geistesgeschichte* vs. History of Ideas," p. 201). As a result, the literary historian who strives to "see as a unity" the historical totality of an age is responsible for his depiction and for his intellectual orientation: the exchange of ideas is a vital part of the "total system" of ideas that constitutes the spirit of a nation.[58] Thus, a Lovejoy is culpable for his adherence to a total system that fails to distinguish Hitlerism from humanism.

113

Since the history of a thing can be established only when it exists in the mind of the historian, it can be seen that Spitzer did not reorder his inner vision and moral priorities in response to the outward reality of a world war. Instead, he forged his subjective version of the state of events, satisfied himself through a holistic click that his perceptions were true, and then projected his personal vision outward upon the actual realm of the world. Thus, the profound problems of the world could be approached through the surface of specific philological debate; an example of this procedure is to be found in Spitzer's "Answer to Mr. Bloomfield (Language 20, 45)" (1944). For Spitzer, a Manichean opposition exists between the mechanism of Leonard Bloomfield and the mentalism which he himself advocates: the mechanist "must avoid such vague terms as 'soul' until [he has] redefined them in terms of biology and sociology"; the mentalist "would not deny that there enters into the latter sciences what he calls the soul."[59] Spitzer endeavors to demonstrate that Bloomfield's position—like Lovejoy's—is erroneous: he provides a variety of language-oriented arguments that weaken, for him, the authority of Bloomfield's theory of language.

But Spitzer is not content simply to refute Bloomfield's ideas point by point, for that would depend upon the analytical perspective one employs to evaluate which scholar is correct. Spitzer's ideas "are folklore only provided Mr. Bloomfield's way of thinking is the truly scientific one—and, conversely, his remarks are linguistic folklore if mine are scientific." No, having penetrated already through the surface to the deep essence of Bloomfield's position, Spitzer *knows*—before writing—the totality of spiritlessness in Bloomfield's stance; thus, the philological circle assigns priority to the inner act of assigning values over the physical act of transcribing these opinions. The crux of Bloomfield's error lies in his attribution to science of atheistic qualities: "After observing the development of science in different countries, I firmly believe, and my years in America have only strengthened this belief, that there can be no real science without faith: religious or metaphysical." Spitzer's reading of Bloomfield's philosophy—that he stands against spirit and humanism—places his opponent in dubious company:

It is not because we do not know the forces active in nature and in man that we are so often unable to prevent catastrophes in both realms, but because of the particular concatenation or the colossal dimensions of circumstances in which the well-known forces appear, and also . . . because our will and imagination too often lag behind our knowledge. And the reduction of the human soul to biology and sociology will do little for mankind; on the contrary, it will undermine the belief of man in himself and thereby bring about catastrophes hitherto unknown to mankind. This lack of belief in man's "himself" has already, in fact, brought about the Hitler catastrophe—which would have been impossible had Hitler's resentment not counted with the automatic and behavioristic, in fact the animal-like, the ape-like and the tameable, in human nature. [60]

In this remarkable passage, Spitzer affirms his notion of Spirit-infused history. Man does have an awareness of the forces in himself and in nature that affect the course of history. We are frequently unable to alter the path of events because those events usually present themselves as being beyond the scope of our mortal conceptualization, or else we are unable to muster the moral character and creative integrity to act in accordance with our insights. In either case, a divine Providence is necessary to complete the process by which events occur in history. To deny the presence of the Divine—as Spitzer believes Bloomfield is doing—undermines man's sense of his nature and leads to disasters such as the Second World War.

Since "nothing stands alone . . . everything is fitted into the Whole . . . represents the Whole," and since "to understand is equivalent to having understood," it is possible to trace Spitzer's thought process as he insists, first, that the repudiation of faith in the world *will* "undermine the belief of man in himself" and usher in "catastrophes hitherto unknown," and then, second, as he holds forth that the catastrophe *has already occurred*; is, in fact, now occur-

115

ring in the guise of the Hitler regime in Germany. Bloomfield, then, is not only in the wrong for forcibly clinging to the malign doctrine that spiritual and physical values must be kept separate—as a particular idea within a discipline; he is blameworthy for the ominous "total system of [his] ideas charged with emotion," which, when "fitted into the Whole," enable us to perceive the dire connections between his specific ideas and the "historical movement" of Hitlerism. Owing to Spitzer's belief that "the idea *and* the word are, at every moment of the reading, *seen* together,"[61] his conclusion is that

the weakening of the idea of God is a signal for the weakening of causal thinking. A monotheistic trend is at the basis of any scientific synthesis. When, on the contrary, the monotheistic pattern . . . disintegrates, everything crumbles; when one has lost the divine, one loses the power of abstraction, one cannot feel, cannot live for, an abstract thought; the table of values collapses; all things stand out unconnected, without halo or lustre . . . the senseless and the mechanic is accepted without scruples; calm wisdom is replaced by a busybody's erudition, understanding by tabulations; books fall to pieces in a world of chaotic minds: the children in school can no longer construct a Latin period, grasp the meaning of a play, explain a line—in short, the picture of our times has already been predicted: . . . Into this picture fits the nihilism of the behaviorists and anti-mentalists who do not know what the soul is.[62]

This lengthy denunciation reveals the extent to which Spitzer relies upon his intuited certainty that (in René Wellek's words) "'all is all,' that everything is related to everything."[63] With Providence encompassing all human life, no random idea or word is ever innocuous: word-ideas constitute the surface through which we may penetrate to the soul of the nation and the essence of truth. From the surface of Bloomfield, Spitzer "clicks" through to the inner reality of the following ultimatum: "our whole civilization" is standing "at the crossroads . . . will it re-establish faith, the basis of all science and of all civic life?" or will it lapse into a doom of massive undifferentiation?[64]

And where—in this polarity between values and nihilism—do we find Spitzer? As a humanist, he lives among his fellow men and will experience any disaster inflicted on mankind; as a philologist, he is detached from the world, "somewhat removed," in order to chronicle human history properly. Thus, Spitzer views himself as an agent of decency who, possessed with a sense of the present and the eternal, transcribes the outer state of the world in order to improve its inner essence: "And yet, by virtue of having been defined, the disharmonious is overcome: disharmony is conquered by the harmony of form."[65] Spitzer's function, then, as he conceives it, is that of the prophet, consistent with his monotheistic tendency "toward the tracing of things to a single origin." Endowed with faith and a divine inspiration, he is the teacher who will lead his people—and accompany them—to the promised harmony beyond. To accomplish his task, Spitzer will exploit his knowledge of and insight into "the human languages . . . each of which strives toward, but never quite reaches, the perfect, supratemporal clarity . . . of the divine language, [which] belong definitely to that part of man that hails from the City of God."[66]

During the Second World War, Spitzer's avowal of the unity between idea and word led him to undertake a variety of linguistic studies: each scholarly article traced the historical derivation of a key word, one that Spitzer believed would lead to a pure and harmonious state of awareness once it was clarified. Spitzer's teacher, Meyer-Lübke, had regarded so-called learned words as subsidiary to the more common words of the "natural language"; Spitzer did not agree, for the philologist-historian needed to express and interact with the cultural aspirations and inner values of the learned public among whom he lived. "Not to deal with the meaning of the learned words means simply to shy away from the whole semantic content of our civilization."[67] Each key word, then, served to initiate the click by which the philologist penetrates to the inner truth of linguistic history; but because words are ideas, the linguist is, as well, a cultural and intellectual historian. An exhaustive etymology of a charged word enables the historian to create history while he preserves it. And because he believed in the balance between word and deed, the permanence in written form of a critical study affirming the harmonious context of a crucial word would do much, Spitzer thought, to establish harmony in the world at large.

Many of these studies—on *Muttersprache* (mother tongue), on *Schadenfreude* (malicious joy), on milieu and ambience, on race, on Gentiles—appeared in *Essays in Historical Semantics* (1948).[68] In "Ratio > Race," Spitzer examines the derivation of that word, *race*, in whose name the Nazis had perpetrated crimes against humanity. As utilized by the Nazis, the concept of racial purity serves to distinguish forcibly between peoples and to set them apart from one another; once it is accepted as scientifically valid, it predicates that humans are relatively superior or inferior, depending upon the degree to which their racial derivation is pure or impure. The Hitleristic usage runs contrary to the humanistic idea of Spirit, which acts to unify peoples and affirm their innate harmony. Thus, Spitzer's insight and then discovery (for that is the order in which the philological circle proceeds) is his evidence to certify that the word which is currently used in opposition to Spirit had itself a high spiritual origin; that the Nazis had based their meaning of *race* on an erroneous interpretation of the original meaning of the word serves to negate the legitimacy on which the fascist authority is based. Spitzer's work demonstrates that the original sense of *race* was based, not on what distinguished between peoples, but on what was held in common. Hence, a humanistic revision of the German text of race is, in actuality, a reestablishment of the purity of the original meaning of *race*: "love, Hope and Faith are here germinal principles: one might say, the spiritual genes of man."[69] For Spitzer, then, the insight into and discovery of the correct derivation of the word *race* helps to undermine the noxious derivation of human ancestry on which the Nazi regime was based. Moreover, to affirm again the harmonious basis of human life is, for Spitzer, a reminder that the antihumanistic fascist *Reich* can be only a temporary aberration.

It should be clear, however, that since the click of understanding precedes the actual work of establishing the proof for that conception, Spitzer *set out* to verify that which he had already intuited. His etymology, then, is not only a discovery, but—considering the political context—a task as well. We should not, however, be tempted to conceive of this sense of motivation as being related to Auerbach's dialectical imperative for historical revision. Spitzer's faith in the symbiosis between word and idea and between word and deed enabled him to hold that the channels of truth flow inherently from one humanistic realm to another.

In "The Gentiles," Spitzer launches another unique investigation into the derivation of a word in order to prove what he already knows to be true. He begins by asking why, since the word *Gentile* refers to one who is not a Jew, Christians would use the word to refer to themselves: to do so "means that they agree to be looked at from without . . . . And why should the Christians include themselves among (indeed, identify themselves with) the heathen, instead of considering themselves as the successors of God's elect people, the Jews, as they have done in former times?" (Spitzer, *Historical Semantics*, pp. 171–72). Furthermore, he asserts that it is curious for the Jewish minority to be discriminated against by a Christian majority that refers to itself as non-Jewish in the United States, while in Nazi Germany the majority "Aryans" spoke of the Jews as "non-Aryans."

The conflict here is between the sense of a word as it is used and conceived of by those who speak it and the absolute, or original, sense of the word's meaning. Another investigative possibility might be to explore what social and cultural factors existed in the United States that might contribute to such a usage of the word. But Spitzer found the usage curious, and that perception provided him with the click of insight; he is striving to prove that insight through the endeavor of seeking the derivation and through the writing of the article. Considering Spitzer's point of origin—that the contemporary usage by Christians in the United States of the word *Gentile* does not seem to be in accordance with the way it should be used—it is not surprising to find that he concludes: "It would then appear that the original emphasis of the antinomic couple "Jews—Gentiles," which is still used by Christians in modern American speech, was not on discrimination between two opposed groups, but on fusion—since discrimination is made meaningless by a higher, a spiritual principle of Christianity (here, of a deistic brand" (Spitzer, *Historical Semantics*, p. 174). Indeed, Spitzer suggests that the Calvinistic American colonists—in their emigration from Europe to the United States— actually identified their plight with that of the biblical Israelites. So an American postwar blight—anti-Semitism—is found to be based on a misnomer and, thus, has no legitimate meaning: it is without reality as a word or deed. To provide final authority for his etymological proposal, Spitzer includes a personal anecdote to assert the veracity of his ideas through his own exemplary life experience: that in the Austria of his youth, *Israelite* was a nonpejorative term for a Jew; so did the Calvinistic settlers identify themselves as Israelites.

When presented with an unfavorable American phenomenon, Spitzer's instinct is to recreate the United States according to his own conception of it and, thus, eliminate the difficulty. Behind a differentiating and discriminatory epithet, Spitzer again finds (or rather, proves what he already knows) a continuity between peoples and cultures, between spirit and history.

Spitzer characterizes all of his word histories as having the particular words for protagonists. But it is important to remember that by words he includes ideas and suggests actions. Further, he holds that for there to be a hero of a history, the history must exist first in the mind of the historian. The word histories, then, constitute a movement toward the pure and original meaning that preceded all derivative meanings. To attain that goal, Spitzer works his way through a variety of aspects which exerted an influence on the words: "The personalities which have left their imprint on the words can only be those of civilizations although these, in turn, have naturally been formed and colored by the personalities of individuals (who, however, were only giving expression to the general feelings of their civilization)" (Spitzer, *Historical Semantics*, p. 1). Words display the influence of civilizations, which were formed by the influence of particular people who, in influencing civilization, tended to exert the effect of a generalized human force.

All of this must be conjured in the mind of the historian Spitzer so that he may experience the click of insight that anticipates his understanding of the word as protagonist which he means to transmit to us. The operational principle is elucidated in Spitzer's study of milieu and ambience as realms of harmony enveloping the world: "And, simply to define an unhappy situation frees us somewhat from its oppression; the formulation of a principle, even a hated principle, partakes of the innate freedom of human thought" (Spitzer, *Historical Semantics*, p. 217). Underlying this passage is the notion that to define—to provide meaning, clarity—is to liberate from an unhappy situation; hence, unhappy situations and their oppression ensue from an absence of meaning, clarity, definition. "In the beginning was the Word, and the Word was with God, and the Word was God" (John 1:1)—thus, for Spitzer, all efforts to make words lucid bring us closer to the spiritual essence (*Geist*) of the universe and its innate harmony. And it is through words and their meanings that it is possible to reattain the harmony which is imperiled during times of crisis.

Spitzer conceived of *Linguistics and Literary History: Essays in Stylistics* (1948) as a foil to *Essays in Historical Semantics* (1948); but instead of letting the words serve as protagonists, he focuses on "individual writers, whose literary personalities are studied in their written words, in their own particular style" (Spitzer, *Historical Semantics*, p. 1). A particular superficial stylistic tendency of the author provides the impetus for the click by which Spitzer penetrates to the inner essence of the author, the society and civilization in which the author functioned, and the culture and world in which Spitzer operates. Each essay, then, may be perceived as an illustration of the means by which one proceeds from a specific stylistic observation to a general expression of thematic vision: "We will be able to penetrate from any peripheral point of the work of art to its core. It is my firm belief . . . that any one good observation will, when sufficiently deepened, infallibly lead to the center of the work of art. There are no preferential vantage points . . . any well-observed item can become a vantage-point and, however arbitrarily chosen must, if rightly developed, ultimately lose its arbitrariness."[70] But the phrases "well-observed," "sufficiently deepened," and "rightly developed" alert us that a prevailing moral refrain encompasses the entire collection of essays.

Displaying the influence of his fellow Viennese citizen Sigmund Freud, Spitzer searches the style of an author in an effort to detect an abnormal variation from the traditional mode; this authorial eccentricity (if it induces the click) is then analyzed to grasp the significance of its breach of literary custom: "The individual stylistic deviation from the general norm must represent a historical step taken by the writer . . . : it must reveal a shift of the soul of the epoch, a shift of which the writer has become conscious and which he would translate into a necessarily new linguistic form; perhaps it would be possible to determine the historical step, psychological as well as linguistic?"[71] But to detect an "individual stylistic deviation from the general norm," one must possess a conceptualization of what the historical general norm was. Since it is clear that our appraisals of the historical general norm, or of the historical "soul of the epoch," are irretrievably entangled with our contemporary conceptualization of our own historical era, our judgments about past general norms are subject to change along with our present norms and values. Did Spitzer hold—after Einstein—that our ability to evaluate is dependent on our particular perspective?

> *Between the idea*
> *And the reality*
> *Between the motion*
> *And the act . . .*
> *Between the conception*

> *And the creation*
> *Between the emotion*
> *And the response*
> *Falls the Shadow.* [72]

So wrote T. S. Eliot in 1925. For Leo Spitzer, between the conception of his intellectual argument and the creation of his critical article, between the click of his esthetic inspiration and the task of his scholarly proof, falls the shadow—and it is a shadow that mediates between the judgments and opinions which Spitzer holds as a man in historical time and the ideals and values that he expresses in time but believes are timeless and eternal. So it is evident that Spitzer does not adhere to a perspectivistic orientation; rather, the ideals and values that he held to be true affect his evaluations about his culture and society; and his present estimation of his world conditions his conceptualization of the historical general norm and the individual stylistic deviation that is determined in relation to it. The larger protagonist behind each of Spitzer's American essays on historical writers and their styles is Leo Spitzer.

In "Linguistic Perspectivism in the Don Quijote," Spitzer isolates the multifarious names provided for several of the characters in the fiction. But because they have come to his attention, "there must be a common pattern of thought behind all these cases." The tremendous variety of names and titles exists, he suggests, because Cervantes wished to emphasize the way in which a person may possess several distinct natures or essences—hence, each name reflects a "different aspect under which the character in question may appear to others." From the click of this realization, Spitzer proposes that Cervantes's world view is based on the same principle: that "the world, as it is offered to man, is susceptible to many explanations." [73] From his absolute vantage point as the novelist, Cervantes was able to depict a fictional world of multiple positions and points of view. He based his perspectivistic novel on the relativity between characters, all controlled by the absolute whim of the author.

The liability of this formulation was cited earlier in Spitzer's criticism of historical relativism: the degree to which everything is relative under its terms. If the author exerts absolute control over the fiction, then who controls the author? and who controls the author's author? etc. This cynical interpretation might follow logically from Spitzer's initial point of penetration. But Spitzer calls a halt to this infinite regress:

Such perspectivism, however, had, in the age of Cervantes, to acknowl-edge ultimately a realm of the absolute—which was, in his case, that of Spanish Catholicism. Cervantes . . . always sees himself as overshadowed by supernal forces: the artist Cervantes never denies God, or His institu-tions, the King and the State . . . Cervantes's God [is] placed above the perspective of language. [Spitzer, *Linguistics and Literary History*, p. 61]

Such an authorial position—absolute mastery of one's art, meek subservience before God—was, Spitzer asserts, unique in the history of literature: never before or since has an author approached his art with such freedom or his world with such reverence for its origin. Modern authors "have failed to sense the unity behind perspectivism . . . in their hands, the personality of the author is allowed to disin-tegrate" (Spitzer, *Linguistics and Literary History*, p. 72).

As our world is increasingly characterized by a decline of humanistic Spirit, so may we perceive the exemplary quality of Cervantes's achievement: his was "no fate-bound dionysiac dissolu-tion of the individual into nothingness and night, as with Schopenhauer and Wagner, but a freedom beneath the dome of that religion which affirms the freedom of the will." In effect, Spitzer is presenting Cervantes to us in order to exclaim: See what is possible when all is in its place, when God is a presence in the world! To reverse the path away from theology, it is crucial that we emphasize moral values in the modern world. Thus, we begin with a specific author and an abnormal stylistic trait and end with the "core" of the work, and of all work, for Spitzer: the wonder of the Word of God and its penetration into all aspects of our human lives. And the prophet who has alerted us to this truth, the man who, like Cervantes, revels in his authorial absolutism but bends before the divine, is Leo Spitzer:

Any philological study must start . . . with the assumption on our part of the perfection of the work to be studied and with an entire willingness to sympathy; it must be an apologia, *a theodicy in a nutshell. In fact, philology has its origin in the* apologia—*of the Bible or of the classics. For philology is born from Biblical criticism and humanistic endeavors, both of them attempts to justify the* So-sein, *the "being so and not otherwise" of exemplary texts. A criticism which insists on faults is justifiable only after the purpose of the author has been thoroughly understood and followed up in detail.* [Spitzer, *Linguistics and Literary History,* pp. 73, 85, 128–29]

In "The Style of Diderot," Spitzer begins with Diderot's "self-accentuating rhythm," a tendency that works against the formal limits of the literary work in which it appears. This stylistic inclination, abnormal when compared with the general classical style, may be attributed to "a certain nervous temperament" that "energize[s] style" (Spitzer, *Linguistics and Literary History*, p. 135). It would appear, then, as if Spitzer were seeking to uncover the essence of Diderot's psychological state. It is certainly true that the essay displays Spitzer's distinctive utilization of Freudian psychoanalytical theory on literature in exemplary form; but it is also true that Spitzer lost interest in literary psychoanalysis immediately after the article was completed ("Precisely the insight that 'psychological stylistics' is not valid for earlier writers . . . has reinforced in me another tendency which was present in my work from the beginning, that of applying to works of literary art a structural method that seeks to define their unity without recourse to the personality of the author. Indeed, the article on Diderot . . . is the last written by me in the Freudian vein").[74] The detection of Diderot's inner essence was never his ultimate objective.

Insight into the core of Diderot's self is insufficient to constitute the type of humanistic epiphany that Spitzer desires to transmit. For

Diderot, "nervous system, philosophical system, and 'stylistic system' are exceptionally well attuned." So his "perpetual desire to transcend the rationally graspable" must coexist with an "urge for self-potentiation," as evidenced by the rhythms of his prose, which Spitzer believes replicate the sexual act.[75] Thus, for Spitzer, Diderot's writing and inner nature provide evidence of automatism. As usual, Spitzer has chosen his term with care; he intends every sense of the word's meaning to be applicable: the idea that human functioning is completely regulated by physical and physiological sources without consciousness as a factor, the uncontrolled movement of an organic activity without direction from the brain, movement or activity without conscious awareness, the process of encouraging the unconscious to display itself through unregulated images. As a result, an affinity is suggested between the historically removed automatism of Diderot and the contemporary mechanism of Leonard Bloomfield, which was discussed earlier.

With this orientation it should not be difficult to perceive that Spitzer's explication of Diderot provides him with a means to comment on the ongoing decline of religion; the psychoanalytical insights into Diderot's authorial self serve as a vehicle by which Spitzer means to propel us to the actual inner core—that automatism is one consequence of a far-reaching disrespect for what is sacred:

It is the absence of the feeling for the divine . . . which has made possible that autonomy of expressivity and that bodily mimicry of thought by speech which leads to the disintegration of thought: when the Spirit of God no longer bloweth whither it listeth, man feels his thought autonomous, and speech, no longer subdued to Logos, becomes predominantly a matter of the body, subject to automatism: something felt in one's veins and nerves. [Spitzer, *Linguistics and Literary History*, pp.167–68]

The dualism that Spitzer envisions for the humanist—between the body which lives among men and the mind which seeks to transcend historical existence in order to write about men—is here apparent. On the one hand, Spitzer is describing Diderot's automatism as a literary historian; on the other, he is delivering a pungent critique of a modern world which has lost its soul, emphasizing the moral values that he feels rise above history. But since the click of the philological method provides the critic with a holistic awareness of the deep content existent in meaning, it should be evident that Spitzer had already realized that "the feverish staccato style was invented by Diderot because he was deaf to the legato of the divine melody" (Spitzer, *Linguistics and Literary History*, p. 168) before he set about obtaining the stylistic evidence necessary for the writing of the article. Hence, his treatment of Diderot serves as a means for him to realize his moralistic refrain. The art of Diderot is, like all art, a surface from which we ascend to a contemplation of the divine.

It is now possible to comprehend the self-congratulatory tonality that distinguishes the end of this article and frequently accompanies the conclusions of Spitzer's other articles. Earlier, Spitzer describes Diderot's awareness of "the amorality which stems from the artistic impulse itself," and presents us with a contemporary example: "the shamelessness of the performer (which prompted, in our times, the tenor Gigli to offer himself immediately to the Allied authorities occupying Rome, with the words: 'I have sung for Mussolini and for the Germans—and now I will sing for you')." But since Diderot's consciousness was forged by his rejection of the divine, it is natural that we retain this awareness when considering the modern anecdote: undoubtedly, it, too, results from the same cause. Having arranged his argument in such a fashion, what does Spitzer mean by this exclamation?

Having come to the end of this article, I ask myself, in all humility, why no previous critic, so far as I know, has been able to formulate clearly the particular Diderotian essence . . . [when] clues to the writer's general artistic intention have been given the critics in "every page and line and letter" . . . and, nevertheless, the critics have not seen the figure in the carpet which repeats itself, with all its circumvolutions, in the work before their eyes! [Spitzer, *Linguistics and Literary History*, pp. 157, 169]

127

Spitzer offers the suggestion that the critics may have been misguided: by their procedure of seeking what is concealed, they were unable to view what was directly before them. Entirely absorbed in the this-worldly nature of the work itself, they sought contrived explanations within the thing, and thus were blind to the otherworldly essence of the work, which emphasizes an awareness of the unity between the here and the hereafter. Only Spitzer is able to see what is before everyone, but which is obfuscated by the darkness accompanying moral distress; only Spitzer, possessing the light of spiritual clarity, is able to perceive the truth, as a prophet among ordinary critics. Like Diderot, the contemporary critics are without a fundamental "feeling for the divine." Spitzer wishes his philological tour de force to attest to the sublime clarity of ethereal vision.

Instead of interpreting an author without faith in order to sound the refrain of faith, Spitzer is more satisfied with the examination of an author with considerable spiritual resources—the Catholic poet Paul Claudel in "Interpretation of an Ode by Paul Claudel." Here, Spitzer begins with one stanza from Claudel's ode and uses—as the point of origin—the repetition of the epithet *grand*. He finds that the rhythms of the lines are in accordance with the repetition; from this, Spitzer decides that "the theme and rhythm must be considered together: the theme is that of gradual ascension and triumph." Spitzer documents in the text the process by which Claudel rises to, and affirms, his religious values. Once his spirituality is embraced, Claudel is able (using a technique that Spitzer credits to Walt Whitman and terms "chaotic enumeration") to catalog the state of modern reality, "in order to evoke the plenitude of the world" (Spitzer, *Linguistics and Literary History*, pp. 193, 206).

Spitzer identifies with Claudel's authorial stance: he sees the poet's commitment to the divine as being akin to the fervid—albeit less doctrinaire—mysticism that he himself seeks to communicate through his philological studies. When armed with such a sustaining creed, the world is recast for the believer and he perceives all things anew:

The more confusing and inchoate our civilization appears, the firmer seems to become the poet's grip on the essentials. But Claudel does not meet the confusion of our world by imposing thereupon a rigid orderliness of his own making: he is able to accept *it without letting himself be distracted from the essentials: he can calmly depict the apparent disorder, for he sees it in a higher order. His faith remains unshaken.* [Spitzer, *Linguistics and Literary History*, pp. 206–7]

With this enunciation, Spitzer sidesteps what was for Auerbach a central dilemma—the relationship between the depicted reality in art and historical reality—and asserts his own crucial opposition: between the historical reality of our world (including art) and that world perceived from the perspective of the essential existence in the hereafter. As an American, Spitzer supports Claudel's positive attitude toward technological change; instead of considering the mechanization of the contemporary world as a threat, Spitzer views it both as a testimony to the influence of the Divinity and as an enthralling challenge for the artist. How does one incorporate technological reality into the form of literary art and, thus, transform it into a thing of beauty? (Spitzer, *Linguistics and Literary History*, pp. 210–11). In this way, the confusion and fragmentation of the modern world are usurped by the clarity of art.

Spitzer's transference toward Claudel is so pervasive that he is moved to equate that poet's achievement with Dante's:

This poetry rivals in factual density that of Dante, while the French poet loses sight as little as the Italian of things eternal. One might say that it is just because these poets have their eyes calmly fixed on eternity that they can portray so well the "man of the world" and the things of their own century: for them (as Auerbach has pointed out in regard to Dante) the fullness of God radiates through the manifoldness of this earth. [Spitzer, *Linguistics and Literary History*, p. 215]

This depiction of Claudel serves well to illustrate Spitzer's self-conception: since he exists within the world, yet serenely contemplates eternity, he is able to penetrate with nonpareiled insight into "the things of [his] own century." Such a conception, however, suggests that Spitzer gauges the value of a work of literary realism by the extent to which its author's "eyes [were] calmly fixed on eternity"; the author's purpose in cataloging the state of the world is used to evaluate the worth of that catalog. In this capacity, the reference to Auerbach is instructive. Auerbach would not have endorsed Spitzer's use of his words; for him, Dante's accomplishment shattered the frame of a religious world view and ushered in a historicistic interpretation of reality. According to Auerbach's "extreme relativism," no modern poet could be equated with Dante, for the modern historical world cannot be compared to Dante's world with its unified Christian perspective.

Spitzer sees—in Claudel's movement from all that is pagan in the world to all that is spiritual—a resistance to the agnostic tendencies of modern history. The forces of science, which previously avoided spiritual truths, are shown by Claudel to be merely another manifestation of the divine: "science and faith are reconciled." Since everything emanates from spirit, the explication of literary reality becomes, ultimately, a matter of form: "A world-poem of today must evidently find a new form, evenly balanced between the conservative and the progressive, reflecting our own time while reminding us of the past" (Spitzer, *Linguistics and Literary History*, pp. 217–18). And such a form encompasses our world in the scope of the beyond.

In February of 1948, Spitzer delivered a series of three lectures on literature at Smith College; those talks were assembled and published as *A Method of Interpreting Literature* (1949). Concerned as they are with disparate literary subjects—the rendition of ecstasy in poetry, Voltaire, and American advertising—Spitzer's use of *method* in the volume's title is again akin to "habitual procedure of mind," rather than a systematic mode of explication. In "Three Poems on Ecstasy (John Donne, St. John of the Cross, Richard Wagner)," he develops the idea that mystical religious ecstasy may be considered as a metaphor for philological interpretation. Typically reactive,

Spitzer begins by responding to the poet Karl Shapiro's contention that poetry has no sense beyond poetry ("it can be understood, paraphrased, or translated only as poetry"). Spitzer's refutation is that poetry—through its language—functions on a dual level: "But there is also to be considered the undeniable fact that *language*, the particular medium of the poet, is itself a system both rational and irrational; it is lifted by him to a plane of still greater irrationalism while nevertheless maintaining its ties with the normal, mainly rational language."[76] Thus, like the humanist who must exist within the world but who must detach himself from it in order to understand that existence, the poet's language both connects him to the world of meaning and—through art—enables him to transcend it.

The poet transforms the mundane words of life into the incandescent words of art, but both senses of the word are preserved: it exists in its standard connotation, but also in its artistic "logic beyond our human logic." Poetry, for Spitzer, "consists of *words*, with their meaning *preserved*, which, through the magic of the poet who works within a 'prosodic' whole, arrive at a sense-beyond-sense; and . . . it is the task of the philologist to point out the manner in which the transfiguration just mentioned has been achieved" (Spitzer, *A Method of Interpreting Literature*, pp. 4, 5). Thus, in opposition to Shapiro, the fundamental concern is not whether poetry is rational or irrational; instead, the process by which it is metamorphosized from one sense to another (while retaining both contexts) is the crucial entity. And the philologist's responsibility is to explicate this movement from sense to "sense-beyond-sense"; it is his obligation to shed light on the twofold function of art. Clearly, the philologist, in Spitzer's view, ought to possess a mystical capacity: the ability to attain an understanding of the sense-beyond-sense and to anchor this comprehension in the reality system of the conventional world.

The philologist, with his circle of understanding, for whom "the first step, on which all may hinge, can never be planned: it must already have taken place"; the philologist who reaches inside himself to obtain the unity that lurks deep within the work of art and its culture; the philologist who believes "that to read is to have read, to understand is equivalent to having understood": how similar is the soul of Spitzer's philologist to "the *mystic* soul . . . able to affirm its knowledge of that individual God . . . as its *personal* possession in isolation, even in secrecy":

Mysticism, indeed, posits privation, renunciation and purgation, as the starting point toward fulfillment: expanding the Christian tenet that to have-not is ultimately to have, that only by closing one's eyes to the outward world does one truly see (the eyes of the heart, oculi cordis, *are keener than the eyes of the senses), and that the light of the heart shines brighter than any other light.* [Spitzer, *A Method of Interpreting Literature*, pp. 30, 31]

But, whereas the mystical experience is an entirely personal one, occurring "in isolation, even in secrecy," the humanistic basis of philology mandates that it spring from the inner source and be communicated and disseminated among men, in order that the serenity of individual communion with the spirit may help usher in a general harmony among human souls.

The mystical ecstasy embodied in the texts of John Donne and St. John of the Cross exemplifies the religious lyricism that Spitzer believes has provided a positive influence on modern civilization—each author presents us with "evidence of the flesh and evidence of time," unified in the moment of "inner feeling." But in Isolde's *Liebestod*, in Richard Wagner's *Tristan und Isolde*, Spitzer perceives a different kind of ecstasy: "for him, the ecstasy of death is a consummation of the ecstasy of love . . . in Wagner's idea of love the craving for death is implied . . . death itself has the quality of erotic ecstasy." Once the figure of God ceases to be the ultimate representation of human dynamics ("to the Church Fathers erotic love was only a lowly reflection of love for God"), then all human aspirations strive toward the carnal. Without the solace of the Deity above us, human individuality is perceived as an unendurable burden; and the comfort of faith is confused with the stillness of death. Such a spiritless world view can only provoke ominous tendencies:

> But underlying the artistic form of Wagner's poetry . . . there is the ultimate formlessness of his philosophy. For the desire to escape from one's individuality, whether through love, through death, or through music—a tendency which has led to tragic consequences in the German history of the 19th and 20th centuries—is an essentially formless and nihilistic desire to succumb to the chaos of the universe. But the mystic philosophy that would preserve and purify the personality, which should be annihilated only before the Creator, is a triumph of inward form over the chaos of the world. [Spitzer, A Method of Interpeting Literature, pp. 45, 54, 55, 56]

The advent of Hitlerism is again associated with the decline of religious values in the world. According to Spitzer's usage, the Creator serves as that function which, through the constant comparison of man and God implicit in religious worship, affirms what is most human in mankind; without him, man tends to mistake the worldly for the divine. Spitzer's philology, then, retains its humanistic affiliation through an enduring refrain that differentiates between what is human and what is eternal. And the philologist concerns himself with the mediation between these realms. The "triumph of inward form over the chaos of the world": Spitzer desired such a victory with a passion. To help effect it, he devised and embraced continuities between religious mysticism and humanistic philology, hoping that the melding of intellectual and spiritual inspiration would contribute to a world of benevolent distinctions and sublime harmony.

In his effort to associate the wild, irreverent, undifferentiated impulses of Wagner with the later "tragic consequences" of modern Germany, in his suggestion that the pantheistic ecstasy of the nineteenth-century Wagner marshaled in the sexual love of death (sadism) of Hitleristic Germany (Spitzer, *A Method of Interpreting Literature*, pp. 52–54), Spitzer treads ground which is precariously similar to that which stimulated his criticism of Arthur Lovejoy described earlier. How could Spitzer incorporate a history of ideas approach here and criticize it elsewhere as being nonholistic? The answer is that, in this case, Spitzer was convinced that Wagner's philosophy represented a grotesque elevation of the temporal to a narcissistic mania which would express itself fatefully in history—in effect, he believed that he saw, with "the light of the heart," the truth in its inward form.

In "American Advertising Explained as Popular Art," Spitzer takes a considerable step toward the confirmation of his American identity. Even the title provides an indication of Spitzer's role as he conceived it: the title might easily have been "American Advertising as Popular Art," in which we are invited to think of the former idea in terms of the latter, but the use of *explained* suggests, first, a conclusiveness—that the relationship will be determined finally and for all time. (Perhaps *revealed* would serve as well.) And someone—an explicator—would be doing the explaining. In effect, the title conveys this sense: "American Advertising Revealed by Leo Spitzer to be Popular Art"; such a formulation solidifies Spitzer's inclination to consider himself the heir to European *Geist*, now at work busily explicating the spirit of the American nation.

As usual, Spitzer begins by pointing out the dearth of serious critical commentary on the subject about which he will write. Advertising has never been analyzed in terms of an artistic tradition; nor has it received a "historical explanation . . . which must, somehow, be related to the American national character and cultural history": the necessity for this relationship emanates undoubtedly from the click that motivated Spitzer to undertake the article. The rationale by which he means to interpret advertising along aesthetic and historical lines argues that commercial prose, although not a serious literary art, "offers nevertheless a 'text' in which we can read, as well in its words as in its literary and pictorial devices, the spirit of our time and of our nation—which are, surely, in their way, 'unmittelbar zu Gott [immediate to God].' To adopt a resentful or patronizing attitude toward our time is, obviously, the worst way to understand it" (Spitzer, *A Method of Interpreting Literature*, pp. 103, 104). Here we encounter an explicit reference to art functioning in the atmospheric environs of the Deity; further, in this statement it is possible to detect Spitzer's early awareness of the healthy principle (so prevalent among contemporary structuralists, poststructuralists, and semioticians) that the world constitutes a text for us to read and recreate. However, Spitzer's eagerness to explicate his world is not based on the relativity of language as an expressive medium or system, but on his wish to delineate the world according to the moral values he held to be absolute.

Spitzer selects, as his text, an advertisement for Sunkist oranges. There is a scenic picture, including orange groves, snow-topped mountains, and a large, orange sun. Inserted into the landscape is a glass of orange juice—inordinately huge—placed among the trees; as a caption, there is "from the Sunkist groves of California / Fresh for you" (Spitzer, *A Method of Interpreting Literature*, p. 105). With insight and ingenuity, Spitzer concentrates on the distortions in size and verisimilitude that characterize the advertisement. He relates the disproportionate glass of orange juice to the exaggerated (in terms of size) depictions of Christ in medieval tapestries; he views the elimination of man from what is actually a man-made process (the orange industry) as an example of poetic selection; he discusses the psychological interpretation of the advertisement as a whole and explores its intended effect on its audience; he considers the precious attitude of the text in terms of other baroque styles in literary history. As a result, the advertisement is placed in an aesthetic and historical context. Yet, Spitzer's intention is to move considerably beyond the advertisement as a literary text: he thinks of the orange juice commercial as a starting point from which he means to penetrate to "the American national character and cultural history."

Does the advertisement represent a cynical attempt on the part of the manufacturers to manipulate a gullible American public? Hardly, since "it is precisely because Americans know reality so well, because

135

they ask to face it, and do not like to be hoodwinked, because they are not easily made victims of metaphysical word-clouds as are the Germans, or of word-fulgurations, as are the French, that they can indulge in the *acte gratuit* of the human word in its poetical nowhere-ness" (Spitzer, *A Method of Interpreting Literature*, p. 121). It is interesting that this statement—which Spitzer offers to us as a truth—does not proceed directly from the course of Spitzer's discussion, but rather is presented as a refutation of an unpleasant implication of the argument. Thus, this information about the nature of Americans is introduced from the outside and is not a feasible consequence of the philological circle.

More convincing is Spitzer's treatment of the *you* in the slogan: he sees it as an indication of our wish to be perceived by another as a coherent self; on another level, it embodies the sense of kinship between the one self who perceives and the other who is perceived. Thus, "the advertiser, while preparing his copy for the general public, thinks the 'you' as an 'all of you'—but intends it to be interpreted as a 'you personally.' " In effect, Spitzer is suggesting an opposition between the American sense of self and the sense of community:

Of all the peoples among whom I have lived, the Americans seem to me most jealously insistent on the right of being addressed as individuals. It is an interesting paradox that the same civilization that has perfected standardization to such a degree is also characterized by this intense need for the recognition of one's personal existence. And this need, which is most acutely in evidence when individuals deal with each other . . . can, evidently, not be ignored even when both parties are anonymous. The concern shown in American advertising for the individual psychology . . . must have deep roots in the American soul. [Spitzer, *A Method of Interpreting Literature*, p. 124]

This is an intriguing proposal, and it does relate to Spitzer's assumption of the dual sense of the "you" in the text; its validity, however, depends on the "seem to me" and "must" that anchor the passage in

Spitzer's subjectivity. But if it is true that everything on this earth proceeds directly from God and will ultimately return to him, and if the creatures and things of the earth may be considered examples of the Lord's artwork, then the man who is infused with spirit will be able to posit truths about those creatures that will not be evident to secular sensibilities.

Since Spitzer has previously intuited (in the click which stimulated the article) that "the concern shown in American advertising for the individual psychology . . . must have deep roots in the American soul," this certainty must be established in accordance with the literary and historical context he is utilizing: hence, he proposes that American advertisements are a product of the American Protestant "preaching mentality . . . which is based on the conviction that every man, possessed as he is of the divine spark of reason . . . has only to be taught what is the good in order to accept it and to pursue it to the ever-increasing perfection of his nature." In fact, Spitzer is certain that modern advertising has "taken over the rôle of the teacher of morals" (Spitzer, *A Method of Interpreting Literature*, p. 126); the direct address of the orange juice commercial ("fresh for you") is analogous to the preacher of earlier days holding forth before his congregation: but contained within this postulated descent from the spiritual to the material is a pervasive cynicism about the moral tenability of the American nation.

Using the Sunkist advertisement as a point of entry, Spitzer delves down to what he believes is the core of meaning about the function of advertising in the American civilization:

The emphasis is on the riches of the earth waiting to be enjoyed by man. In a secularized, laicized civilization, where human activity in pursuit of material welfare is not shunned but accepted as a blessing from God, it was easily possible for the mysticism of the pastor's "for you" to become diluted: material welfare, too, could be seen as something willed by God "for you," "for me," personally; there is only a small step from the optimistic preaching of the boundless, the paradisiac possibilities of divine goodness which man must only be ready to accept, to the optimistic preaching of the boundless, the paradisiac possibilities of earthly well-being which, likewise, man must simply allow himself to enjoy. [77]

On the face of it, this is a disparaging passage, for it casts aspersions on the ability in the United States to differentiate between what is lofty and divine and what is crass and mundane. To suggest that self-seeking advertisers have taken over the function of setting moral standards in the United States is to offer a wry and pessimistic observation about the American soul. At the very least, Spitzer is depicting a nation with a hedonistic mentality, occupied with the temporary satisfaction of superficial impulses. Such an inherently cynical conclusion might easily be the cause for grief in comparing the present with the past. (Certainly, Auerbach was inclined to view the modern world from this stance.) Yet despite the nature of his solemn perception about his country, Spitzer's tone in the passage is positive and exuberant: this is because his faith in both his personal integrity and his intellectual gifts, together with his confidence in their elite ability to reveal the ultimate truth, remains untarnished. In his mind, America yields itself to his quest for insight and higher understanding—America becomes "Spitzerized" and, thus, reveals itself to be explicable and under control.

Indeed, Spitzer's exorbitant effort to bolster his postulations about American civilization moves him to assert that the advertisers constitute a primary force in an ideal American society—that they, in fact, exert a positive influence:

American advertising thus becomes one of the greatest forces working to perpetuate a national ideal: in their own way the pictures of happy family life or of private enjoyment have a conservative function comparable to that of the statues in the old Greek Polis; though the American images are not embodiments of gods and heroes, they preach an exemplary well-being as an ideal accessible to every man in the American community. [78]

This lavish attribution of the constructive contributions achieved by

American advertising, this glorification—by a man who is concerned with the dissemination of spiritual virtue in the modern world—of those institutions that bolster man's inclination to possess perishable and vulgar things seems rather skewed and distorted. But it is well to remember that immigrants—especially from violent and oppressive countries—often express extravagant praise for the prodigious blessings of the United States. In his glorification, Spitzer is heeding a familiar tendency to evaluate his adopted country with benevolent eyes. Further, the climate of postwar America fostered the declaration of patriotic sentiments and encouraged the coining of interpretations that furthered nationalistic enthusiasm. It was thought that, in this way, American democracy would be nurtured after the long struggle against fascism and supported for the impending confrontation with communism. In a sense, then, Spitzer's abundant testimonial for American advertisers does reflect the soul of the United States at the time of its composition.

But this is to propose a perspectivistic mode of analysis. Did not Spitzer—in his notion that the humanist must remain in the world but simultaneously detach himself from a subjective stance in order to gauge historical truth—believe that his penetration to the inner soul of a nation would yield a permanent and absolute knowledge? The answer is yes, but it is not until the final paragraph of the article that we find evidence of Spitzer as an objective historian. In devising his conclusion, he is motivated to balance his sense of the United States assembled from his experience as a new American citizen with his sense of the United States derived from his conception of himself as a humanist who "stands at the window of our national civilization before which opens the vista of other civilizations. And he *is* that window, which looks outside, not into the room."[79]

Spitzer's humanistic perspective presents a different appraisal of American advertising:

But, in the interstices between paradisiac dreams and harsh reality, the gracious and gratuitous flowers of poetry, aware of their own unreality,

139

spring up here and there, offering glimpses of an oasis in the aridity of a modern mechanized and pragmatic world. Thus our advertisement designed to promote the retail sale of oranges, offers a colorful image of quiet Nature to refresh the city dwellers in their environment of hustle and drabness. [80]

In this passage, he returns to his idea of the dual function of poetry—both mundane and magic—expressed earlier in "Three Poems on Ecstasy." But here poetry, or art in general, is drawn as the provider of scant spiritual sustenance for a bleak, morally decimated, dehumanized world—here, its dual function, as it were, lies in mediating between a harsh world of "hustle and drabness" and the ethereal serenity of the world beyond. Our society is so undernourished spiritually, according to this view, that even the minimal and distorted art included in a materialistic advertisement provides emergency supplies for a famished society. But it is only by balancing Spitzer's desolate assessment of the United States with his cheery one that we gain an "understanding of the well-motivated, coherent, and consistent organism which our civilization is," as he meant us to do. [81]

As Spitzer's years of residence in the United States increased, so, too, did his identification of himself as an American; the extent to which he became acclimated to his new country influenced the degree to which he began to equate the ideals of the United States with his personal ideals as a historian and philologist. Accordingly, the philologist-historian who was striving to penetrate to the soul of the nation from an entry point within a literary work of art often, without fully realizing it, initiated his circle of understanding with an insight about the soul of the nation derived not from the literary text, but from his own experience as a new American citizen; the scholarly materials would then be arranged to support this encompassing knowledge. To be sure, Spitzer allowed for this factor when he insisted that the personal experience of the critic helped account for his determination of a point of origin and for his ability to perceive a click, but he always emphasized that the deep truth about the inner core logically followed from the click obtained from the literary surface. Perhaps it was because of his intuitive realization of the new interrelationship between Spitzer the American citizen and Spitzer the detached humanist that he tended to react in a testy and defensive manner to questions about his critical procedure. Responding to René Wellek and Austin Warren's discussion of his work in their *Theory of Literature*,[82] Spitzer writes: "I find, in spite of their friendly attitude toward my work, my activity in the field of stylistics somewhat distorted." This inspires a long defense in footnote form, steadily building in emotional intensity and irritability of temperament, until:

I challenge Messrs. [René] Wellek and [Austin] Warren to show that the evidence from which I start . . . is not pure "linguistic material," but conclusions derived from a previous "psychological and ideological analysis" and that either the linguistic evidence . . . or its analysis . . . are "strained" or "based on very slight evidence. . . ." It is a pity that critics of critics . . . fall into the most familiar trap of critics in general: not to understand what they criticize and thus to allow themselves an ultimately sterile fault-finding attitude, thereby making necessary tedious rectifications on the part of critics of the "critics of critics."[83]

It is not that Spitzer does not realize "the dangers inherent in all *explication de texte*: impressionistic overinterpretation, entailing a secondary lyricism of the critic's own making,"[84] it is that he does not believe himself liable to those dangers. For Spitzer, any "lyricism" resulting from "overinterpretation" is excess, but the critic's lyricism in the service of truth is essence.

When Spitzer deals with Walt Whitman in *"Explication de Texte Applied to Walt Whitman's Poem 'Out of the Cradle Endlessly Rocking' "* (1949), he notes: "Since I have no thorough acquaintance with Walt Whitman's sources, I am forced to place him, not within the framework of his American *ambiente*, but somewhere in the cold space of world literature . . . as one among other poetic monuments belonging to the Western tradition." This might be problematic, for Spitzer admits that he does not know whether Whitman was aware of the Western tradition Spitzer will develop; but since his experience has led him to take this stance toward Whitman, his talent and faith will see him through to the inner core. Hence, his conceivable intellectual limitation is revealed to be an advantage: "for I feel that the direct, concrete sources which may be established for a particular work of art are generally somewhat petty and trivial in comparison with the parallels to be found in international art, together with which the particular work combines in an eternal pattern."[85] We may be sure, however, that if Spitzer were possessed with "direct, concrete sources" about a particular work of art, he would not view that knowledge as being "petty and trivial"; rather, he would consider his specific information as a unity with the eternal pattern "to be found in international art"—but when he did not count a specialized source among his vast array of literary accomplishments, then he held it to be irrelevant to the inner truth.

Spitzer's expert analysis arrives at the climactic end of the poem, when the narrator hears:

> . . . *the low and delicious word death,*
> *And again death, death, death, death,*
> *Hissing melodious . . .*
> *My own songs awaked from that hour,*
> *And with them the key, the word up from the waves,*
> *The word of the sweetest song and all songs,*
> *That strong and delicious word which . . .*
> *The sea whisper'd me.* [86]

Spitzer notes that "it is to Whitman that has been revealed the musical meaning of the world, the chord formed by Eros and Thanatos, the infinite cosmos created from infinite chaos, and finally, his own microcosmic role in the creation. It is the knowledge of death that will make him the poet of life, of this world, *not* of the Hereafter." In this lyrical passage, Spitzer comments on the narrator's discovery of a creative artistic source as a result of hearing the voice from the sea. But despite his eloquent poetic explication, he is not blind to Whitman's use of the words "delicious," "melodious," "sweetest," "song" to describe death: he relates Whitman's usage to the eroticization of death prevalent in the work of Wagner and Baudelaire, anticipating the more pronounced manifestations of the tendency in Victorianism, the Second Empire, and "the *fin de siècle* generation . . . when the theme of love-death . . . finally became the theme par excellence."[87]

This is an astute observation: to link three artists who lived during the same age but who were of different nationalities according to a recurring thematic inclination, and then to trace the theme as it affected the artistic stance of subsequent generations—such a study might reveal quite a bit about the relation between literary history and nationalism, for instance, or might suggest a history based on modes of thought. But Spitzer is not interested in developing his comparison. Indeed, because of his emerging identification of his mind and intellectual spirit with the force and principles of the United States, Spitzer desires, as an American, to affirm the unique quality of the American poet Whitman over similar European poets. And since it is through the work of the poet that the nation's soul is revealed, Spitzer is emphasizing the distinctive spirituality of the American soul over its more morbid and perverse European counterparts: "But Whitman, unlike his two sickly European contemporary confrères, will remain for us not the poet of death (although the idea of death may have perturbed him more than once), but the unique poet of American *optimism* and love of life, who has been able, naturally and naïvely, to unite what in other contemporary poets tends to fall apart, the life of man and that of nature."[88]

It is true that, earlier in the article, Spitzer examines facets of the Whitman poem in terms of an overall harmony between man and nature; still, he does not explain why Whitman's incontestably erotic images of death at the end of the poem reflect an "optimism and love of life," while similar images in Baudelaire and Wagner (discussed

143

by Spitzer earlier) reflect a septic decadence. It is not that Spitzer is incorrect in his assessment of Whitman and the American soul; but it is evident that his observation and conclusion—or his inner truth— seem, in this instance, to be grafted to the body of the argument. They are the creations of a moral sensibility so severe that it advocates the influence of "the invisible direction of the critic": Spitzer believes "that the timing of allusions to extraneous elements should be carefully devised."[89] If this exposes a certain rigidity coexisting with his critical intuition, with his impulsive subservience before the literary text, then it also displays the incisive courage of his moral convictions.

Spitzer's faith in a world destiny of harmony and serenity is overwhelming; in the face of historical or literary evidence to the contrary, he seeks to "fight [his] way to his unity." We have already encountered Spitzer's moving and ambivalent portrait of the American soul as it is evoked through the surface of advertising. In the face of similar contradictory evidence about the Whitmanesque American soul it is not surprising for Spitzer to conclude that "Whitman's world-embracing vision is able to contain in itself opposite aspects of the world at once together." But then Spitzer asserts that "we should keep in mind that Whitman's pantheistic unification of the cosmos, as is true of all similar modern attempts, is informed by a pantheism that comes *after* Christianity, a pantheism-that-has-absorbed-Christianity. The Christian feeling for the unity of the world in God can never be lost in modern times, not even when God Himself is lost."[90] We are faced with the expression of a man whose mystical fervor for spiritual unity transcends even the words by which men are meant to comprehend such a dream.

The pantheism Spitzer evokes—that man and the earth are apparitions of a transcendental Deity—accommodates the idea that "opposite aspects of the world" may be "contain[ed]" within a "world-embracing vision," provided that such a vision is in accordance with the original, surpassing unity that is God. Distinctions constitute the temporal surface through which the enlightened eye may perceive the underlying oneness of mortal existence; hence, "all philology rests on the assumption that all men on earth are basically alike and that the modern commentator is enabled, by his training and studiousness, to approximate and, perhaps, restore, the original 'meaning' of a work of art composed at another time and place."[91] But if the work of art expresses the values of the civilization in which it was created, and if history records the process by which civilizations change, it ought to be evident that philology stands as the discipline that perceives differentiation through the guise of an ephemeral unity of momentary perspective. On what, then, does the claim of human identicalness rest? And how may this human identicalness be recognized by the "modern commentator" who is himself a feature of a world of endless permutation? The answer is contained in Spitzer's belief that "poetry is the form best fitted to convince man emotionally of supernal verities. Apperception of poetry may be, then, to a certain extent, religious service."[92]

The homogeneity of human life on earth may be understood only to the extent by which man has allowed the poetic, the religious, the spiritual to become a part of his life. Through the conscious realization of poetry in our lives, we are brought closer to the "supernal verities"—unity, harmony, serenity, peace—that exist as expressions of the divine on earth. Thus, "the Christian feeling for the unity of the world in God can never be lost in modern times, not even when God Himself is lost," because it is the *feeling* for the unity of the world in God—the feeling, the nuance, the style of that unity—that is itself tantamount to the unity of the world in God.

Spitzer's sense that the United States' goals and values best embodied his feeling for the unity of the world in God was the motivating force behind his address to the Modern Language Association in New York on December 28, 1950. In it, he calls for a unification of the best features of the Old World and the New World: he desires that the idea of an intellectual elite (indigenous to the intellectual tradition of Austria and Germany) be incorporated within the American Academy (with its democratic intellectual tra-

145

dition). In this fashion, the humanistic spirit of Europe will be blended with the humanistic spirit of the United States, replicating, as well, Spitzer's own mental adjustment as he moved from Europe to America. Although he suspects that the notion of an elite runs contrary to the basic institutions of American democracy, he is convinced that an intellectual elite will best remedy the faults present in the American university system. Rather than dismissing his plan to link the two systems as hopeless because of the irreconcilable differences between elitism and democracy, Spitzer is resolved to formulate an enduring unity; the two ideas must be seen *"together*: an elite within a democracy—whereby the weaknesses of the latter may be greatly repaired, and the dangers of the former rendered negligible . . . we *will be able* to integrate an elite into our democracy."[93] Here Spitzer dismisses the disturbing connections between elitism and totalitarianism; instead, he diagnoses the American university system as being deficient (in the caliber of scholars produced, in the lack of reverence for the Spirit in our humanistic heritage, in the excessive competition blocking serious study), and concludes that the remedy *must* exist within his own background and past experience. His powerful and mystical assurance that such a unity is inevitable appears more as a prophetic pronouncement than as a viable theoretical proposal. For Spitzer, the force of his own idealism creates a commanding argument. The United States is remade according to his own enlightened vision: the intellectual tradition that influenced Spitzer is preserved within his adopted country. But for the audience of American scholars, who listened to Spitzer's passionate remonstrance without the beneficial support of his linguistic and philological evidence, there may have been many perplexed faces.

The United States at that time was immersed in a process of self-examination: looking backward, in an effort to comprehend the fascism that was recently defeated; looking forward, in an effort to understand the communism that was emerging as the new opponent; looking inward, in order to redefine all forms of totalitarianism and to purge such noxious influences from the nation. Accordingly, suggestions that the American system be modified—no matter how slight the change or congenial the suggestion—were often met by an acutely defensive attitude.

As an American, Spitzer is aware of this gingerly atmosphere within the country; he suspects that his advocacy of an elite will precipitate considerable irate debate and rebuttal. In order to avoid such a response, he phrases his appeal carefully:

You may have decided that, given my criticism of the life actually led by our young scholars in our university system, a system so intimately connected with national ideals, I am criticizing these ideals themselves and that, consequently, as the phrase goes, "I should go back where I came from." But I do not wish to go back, I wish to stay in this country which I love. Is it not understandable that a relationship deliberately based on choice may inspire, at the same time, more passion and more criticism than an inherited relationship? It is just because I find in American democracy the only air in which I could breathe, because I am convinced that the average American is more decent, less selfish, and more human than the average of any other nation where I have lived, that I would wish the American university system to possess all the advantages of the best systems of the old world! [94]

It is not difficult to gauge within this passage Spitzer's opinion that Americans in 1950 possessed a limited appetite for self-criticism; even more apparent is Spitzer's profound faith in his own enlightened vision, in his personal ability to educate a group of scholars about the unity between the old and the new, the historical and the eternal. Essential to Spitzer's faith is his commitment to *"rethinking, reunderstanding* the old. The old is not dead; the old is alive for the man who looks at it with new eyes."[95] And it is the light from above that enables one to see with "new eyes," with the clarity of revelation. Everything is preordained: political events dictate that Spitzer emigrate to the United States; thus, he "find[s] in American democracy the only air in which I could breathe." As an emissary of humanistic values and harmony between men, he takes up residence in the United States; as a result, when he examines his countrymen, he finds that "the average American is more decent, less selfish, and more human than the average of any other nation where I have lived." Spitzer's vision is afire with the clarity of "supernal verities"; such is the measure of his devotion that he seeks to interpret the world in accordance with the truths he holds constant. The United States is to be seen with new eyes so that the old—and eternal— humanistic traditions will merge with the new and be preserved forever.

In order to communicate more extensively with the especially human, decent, and generous American public, Spitzer accepted an invitation to contribute an essay on language to his colleague George Boas's *Studies in Intellectual History* (1953). Without an overt intellectual error to rectify, Spitzer's essay ("Language—The Basis of Science, Philosophy and Poetry") presents a moderate and complacent tone in opposition to the often feisty demeanor of his critical articles and reviews. It is as if Spitzer, in attempting to disseminate his conception of a harmonious world vitalized by the beauty of literary art, were overcome with the serenity of his vision and the possibility of a sensitive perception of that vision by the special American public.

Throughout the essay, Spitzer invokes "the general human mind," "a general human attitude," and "our general human experience" in an effort to integrate his particular humanistic Spirit with the postwar idealistic yearning for world peace that helped create the United Nations. But he does not forget his appraisal of the American public. The philological circle is embraced not only as an explicative method with roots in European humanism, but as:

the method by which all deciphering and even modern decoding techniques are guided—and if the work of American counter-intelligence in the last war that was able to save thousands of lives, has demonstrated to the whole nation a possibility of practical application of the humanities, an applica-

bility which was equal to that of the sciences (if not equally advertised), it must be remembered that our counter-intelligence experts were using the methods of Homeric textual criticism.[96]

In a sense, Spitzer is here exploiting his earlier insights about American advertising in order to "sell" his philology to the American public-at-large. The passage functions as an appeal to American patriotism—it was philological "textual criticism" and explication that provided the means for our "counter-intelligence experts" to uncover the secret (and, therefore, concealed) truth lurking beneath the deceptive surface and, in the process, helped win the great war against fascism. Spitzer is aware, of course, that as Germans, the Nazi counterintelligence agents were heir to explication of the text as well. Had they won the war, their use of textual criticism might have contributed to a dubious cause. But for Spitzer, everything emanates from above. The Nazis did not adhere to a humanistic philology; their spirit was a deceitful one, hence they were doomed to failure. The superior moral fortitude of the United States and the Allied cause—aided by a humanistic textual criticism—guaranteed their victory. The unique American public should be made to realize that the nation's preserved freedom and postwar prosperity are vindications of Spitzer's humanistic philology and its benevolent Spirit.

Even for Spitzer, however, the current situation is less than harmonious. Although the war should have established a firm and easily justifiable respect for the humanities, he still perceives there to be, on the part of Americans, an opposition between the humanities and the sciences. And he believes this polarity exists because Americans view the sciences as being part of the material world while the arts are felt to dwell close to their loftiest spiritual aspirations. In his effort to reestablish a unity between the arts and the sciences under the auspices of the divine spirit, Spitzer again refers to the popular culture of the United States. All men possess "the desire for illusion, for surcease from the laws of causality is indeed deep-rooted in all of us: On the lowest level, in an age of mass civilization and of timidity of imagination, this desire will send many to the comic strips which give them the disinterested enjoyment of a world which, while freed from the modern implications of determinism and transfigured by the comic spirit or the spirit of adventure, can still somehow be felt to be *their own world.*" On a more elevated plane, men find in great literature (such as Dante) "an *entirely imaginary* world with a physics and a biology quite aberrant from our own," whose laws are the laws of God. The challenge, then, is how to reveal the truth that both science and art are in harmony and under the luminous control of the Deity. After all, "there has not yet appeared a modern Dante who would make modern science sing" (Spitzer, "Language," pp. 91, 92).

Until such a modern sage appears, we are left with our language and its possibilities. For Spitzer, it is a rich vein because: "language is not only a banal means of communication and self-expression, but also one of orientation in this world: a way that leads toward science and is perfected by science, and on the other hand also a means for freeing us from this world thanks to its metaphysical and poetic implications" (Spitzer, "Language," p. 93). Science, grounded in the practical reality of the world, comic strips, and other popular art, set in a realistic "near-world," and literature, located in an imaginary alternative world where "it is love that moves the sun and the stars . . . in the presence of God" (Spitzer, "Language," p. 92): all of these express partial mortal representations of the vision of God. All of them, as well, are created through the medium of language—and it is Spitzer, as a linguist, philologist, and literary historian, who sees his task as serving to guide the various users of the language in history toward the primeval unity of men and tongues that he believes preceded history.

So it is that in this essay, with its more accessible style, aimed toward a broader popular audience, Spitzer again finds himself offering a prophetic assurance of the intrinsic unity of the world: "It is my personal feeling that the concepts of the moral world, of God and Devil, will not be abandoned altogether in the centuries to come, but will gradually be rephrased and shaded in consonance with our scientific knowledge of the physical world" (Spitzer, "Language," p. 93). It *will* ensue: through the Word, which contains all things and by which all is revealed, the moral world shall be perceived as being in harmony with the physical world. All differences shall be resolved ultimately since *"language*, the main vehicle for communication of meaning in the business of this world, is able to transform itself into the rainbow bridge which leads mankind toward other worlds where meaning rules absolute" (Spitzer, "Language," p. 93). Here the striving for perfection of form in literature is made analogous to the aspiration for sublimity of spirit in heaven. Thus, Spitzer's search for perfection of form in art, history, and spirit may be viewed as consistent with what he would later describe as "the Jewish metaphysics of history": "All injustice in this world is an interlude between the once perfect state of the world and the final reëstablishment of justice."[97]

Spitzer's attempt to simultaneously guide and be a part of his contemporary society reveals the extent to which he—as a philologist explicating authors whose work he thought depicted the inner truth of their nation and civilization—embodies the mentality of the United States during the fifties. Spitzer's equation of "the methods of Homeric textual criticism" with American patriotism and American counterintelligence efforts may be related to the cache of secret microfilm documents concealed in a pumpkin ("the pumpkin papers"), and the hidden typewriter. Those implements of language, discovered and analyzed, revealed an inner reality beneath the surface of respectability that helped incriminate Alger Hiss during his trial and conviction for perjury (1948–50). Whatever judgments one holds about the case, it was an effort to utilize language in the pursuit of justice, to penetrate beneath the superficial exterior of a man (and, in the controversy surrounding the trial, a political principle) to arrive at the truth. A further impetus for Americans to adopt the notion that nothing is as it seems was contained in the Rosenberg case (1950–53). An irregularly cut Jello box top was one of the pieces of evidence by which the government attempted to establish that beneath their drab, ordinary exterior, Julius and Ethel Rosenberg were spies who had leaked the secret of the atom bomb. Again, regardless of any ultimate evaluation of the case, Americans following the trial were exposed to the idea that truth lurks beneath the facile surface—one must bore under the external appearance of reality to obtain the pure, inner truth.

Indeed, the cold war tensions and the prevailing menace of nuclear destruction occasionally moved Spitzer to temper his fervent optimism about the future possibilities for Spirit in the world. He examined modern attitudes of "relativity" and of "all coherence gone" and concluded that the threat was "not nearly as frightening to the first Renaissance thinkers as it is to our modern so-called 'one world' which again tends to become a boxed-in world, the finite world of Einstein which also includes 'one death,' atomic death."[98] Even the American experience of McCarthyism appears in Spitzer's writing. In "The Individual Factor in Linguistic Innovations" (1956) he discusses McCarthy's "ill-famed" influence in coining new words; Spitzer suggests that the faddishness of the expressions is due to the historical unreliability of the senator's beliefs. When viewed in the light of subsequent history, McCarthy's coinages do not reflect a sound American moral ideal and, thus, are disappearing from popular usage.[99] It is interesting to consider that one popular essayist proposed that McCarthy's accusatory lists of supposed communists embodied "the 'plain man's' conviction that figures are useful only for bolstering after the fact an intuitive judgment or insight."[100] But if Spitzer ever read the essay, it is clear that he did not relate the intuitive judgment supported by figures in the one case with his own intuitive click of insight supported by scholarly evidence that constituted his philological circle; otherwise, we may be sure that he would have written an article attesting to the moral integrity which distinguished his intellectual method from the senator's casual and belligerent charges.

When Spitzer did encounter a valid attempt to use the philological circle, he responded with an aggressive criticism, "A New Book on the Art of *The Celestina*" (1957). He attacks Stephen Gilman in his use of "the method of the 'philological circle' advocated by me for many years. But the success of this method is predicated upon the correct interpretation of the detail first singled out by the critic—and already in this elementary stage Mr. Gilman seems to me to have failed." Here, Spitzer all but admits that his system is best considered when it is functioning in Spitzer's hands. Later he attacks Gilman's assertion that Gilman's interpretation is based on an "intuitive revelation": "We miss here a reference to logic and criticism as tools for the scholar; he speaks as a poet would." Spitzer's vehement resistance to Gilman's use of the philological circle impels him to devise a mature statement of the Spitzerian circle: "Sensitivity for aesthetic values, associative and imaginative powers, learning, the striving toward synthesis, all of them invaluable gifts for a scholar in the humanities, come to naught unless built upon a solid ground of average human experience."[101] The concern for a "solid ground of average human experience" accounts for Spitzer's sensitivity to many of the major cultural and political aspects of his time.

But therein lurks a difficulty. As a humanist who lives physically among his fellow men, but who also detaches himself intellectually from them, Spitzer vigorously attempts to ground himself solidly in the average human experience at the same time that he is striving to define what constitutes an *average* human experience. One ought to determine a criterion by which to establish a meaning for *average* initially; then, having done so, one might proceed to ground oneself in that determined realm of experience. Despite his regard for logic, Spitzer seeks to accumulate average experience before he has fully ascertained what he means by average—or rather, because of his faith and moral integrity, Spitzer believes that what he has experienced, in the light of his insight, reveals and constitutes an average human experience. Thus, Spitzer's procedure is dependent, ultimately, on his "reading" of average America, just as it is his philological circle that enables him, initially, to examine the United States through its constituent literary manifestations.

Spitzer's last years were devoted to the expansion and revision of a linguistic word study which had been published originally in 1944–45. That Spitzer would again be motivated to investigate the derivation of the word *Stimmung* (tune, mood, humor, frame of mind) may be accounted for by his mature belief that

the most important requirement for historical understanding is the philological re-enactment of such world-embracing concepts, which must be sought out in all the nooks and corners of our languages and our civilization. It is not the fact that a certain concept was paramount in a certain civilization that matters most, but the way in which it was present at various times: the way in which its influence made itself felt in details. To state a historical truth about a philosophical concept is not enough. . . The concepts must be taken seriously—as I am obviously attempting to do in the following chapters. [102]

The word itself is no longer simply the protagonist of Spitzer's study, rather, he calls for the "philological re-enactment" of the evolution of the concept that surrounds the word through history. Such a process will support our "historical understanding," but Spitzer is here alluding to something more extensive: he means to move beyond one of the central historicist principles—the understanding "that a certain concept was paramount in a certain civilization"—in order to affirm "the way in which [a concept's] influence made itself felt in details." Thus, it is not only the attainment of an inner core of meaning that is significant for the philologist, but an awareness of the particular manifestations of that meaning in the form of details, grounded in historical reality, considered across historical time. The linguist-philologist becomes not only the chronicler of a word's historical derivation, he becomes the historian of a concept's verifiable existence. To seek out "in all the nooks and corners of our languages and our civilization" the details which establish the existence of a "world-embracing concept" is to assert that the concept is still alive and viable as a presence in the world. If it is possible to pursue an influential concept back to its origins by means of its

154

surviving trace-details, then the concept remains influential and is thus preserved. Through the philological reenactment of a concept as fundamental as world harmony, Spitzer hopes that he may be able to help realize the actuality of an idealized wish. For this reason, "the concepts must be taken seriously."

Spitzer's *Classical and Christian Ideas of World Harmony: Prolegomena to an Interpretation of the Word "Stimmung"* (published posthumously in 1963) exploits a chronological development in order to embrace a world vision devoted to synchronism.[103] It is no accident that the word *interpretation*, rather than *derivation* or *history*, appears in the title as a description of the work, for Spitzer's conscious intention is to transmit the world harmony that he is investigating. He wants his public to consider—all at once—a complex of ideas developed across time under a variety of circumstances. He desires, after Goethe, that we "think again what has once been thought" so that mankind may adopt a "harmonizing habit of thought" (Spitzer, *Classical and Christian Ideas*, pp. 3, 4). In effect, he seeks—through a literary ritual that reenacts history—to transcend the consequences of human history and regain the ephemeral serenity that existed before time, will again exist, and, for Spitzer, has always existed as an embodiment of faith.

Such a study ranks historical theorization as secondary to the rite of apperception of details: the details that act to establish, within our consciousness, the concept of world harmony. Accordingly, Spitzer sketches in his thesis—that world harmony is a function of a "homogeneous [spiritual] 'field'"; that such a unified spirituality existed during pagan antiquity and thrived through centuries of Christianity until "the epoch of dechristianization (from the seventeenth century on), in which our field is radically destroyed" by the attitude of the Enlightenment (Spitzer, *Classical and Christian Ideas*, p. 76)—but places his emphasis on the cumulative effect of the sheer amassing of details demonstrating world harmony. Whereas Auerbach labored to construct an elaborate historical interpretation that would resound mightily against the political circumstances of his age, Spitzer views history not as an imperative, but as an occasion for the display of conceptual details, whose aggregation, he feels, will modify the moral values of the readers who dwell on them. Thus, society will move gently to reestablish the harmony it once enjoyed.

Spitzer's demeanor here reflects his self-ordained role as the purveyor of Spirit. Everything is encompassed by the surrounding harmony; no impediment of resources is sufficient to mar the intellectual unity of the presentation. At one point in the text, Spitzer wishes to cite a number of medieval sources in Italian; none, however, are available to him. Instead, he proceeds to examine Renaissance texts of Spanish. Spitzer's justification for this "extraordinary procedure" is that "Spain, in its literature and its art, was slower than Italy (or France) to dissolve its ties with the Middle Ages . . . what exists in Spain in the seventeenth century, must have existed in the sixteenth in Italy" (Spitzer, *Classical and Christian Ideas*, p. 111). In short, Spitzer erects a colossal verbal edifice to explain the simple fact (and to avoid the consequences of that fact) that the texts he needs are not available to him. And why should a few texts in particular be essential to his argument when he has already intuited the enduring contours of his "world-embracing concept"?

As an example of world harmony, Spitzer considers the "concert of the stars." Here, presenting music devoted to the praise of God under the evening sky, art, nature, and spirit are unified: "The 'concert of the stars' . . . was but a consequence of the topos of world harmony. And underlying this cosmic 'concert' are the associations of order, *consensus*, harmony, peace, 'numbers,' the reflection of world harmony, of its Institutor and Ruler, and of love inspiring His praise" (Spitzer, *Classical and Christian Ideas*, p. 117). But as the consciousness of mankind became increasingly secular during the modern age of our civilization, the concert of the stars lost its predominantly religious context. In its place Spitzer finds classical music, which, since it is performed indoors in a concert hall, and since it offers an abstract art largely devoid of a religious context, he sees as an inappropriate replacement. Also existing, but in "relative unpopularity," is opera, which he rates unacceptable in its present state with "its suggestion of an aristocratic pattern, once a feature of actual life . . . but no longer at hand, even for the very rich, to offer a pretext of reality" (Spitzer, *Classical and Christian Ideas*, p. 124).

All along, Spitzer has been discussing world harmony in terms of its religious and spiritual emphasis: it is through the vision of God that man gains insight into the unity of his existence on earth among other beings; but the portion of his dual-humanistic self that has lived and interacted with people wishes to present evidence selected from his contemporary American environment. Accordingly, the essential spiritual and religious theme is momentarily deemphasized: "Perhaps, if the opera could abandon the outworn baroque and courtly tradition, while still preserving its essential motif of love and music, we would find that the theme of world harmony, musically and dramatically portrayed, has not entirely lost its appeal" (Spitzer, *Classical and Christian Ideas*, p. 124). For the moment, "love and music" seem to be all that is essential for world harmony. But how is this possible for Spitzer? Why has he made the supposedly all-important theme of Spirit so diminutive?

The answer is that Spitzer, as we have seen, equates the American nation and society with the potentiality for Spirit in the world. The United States, with its bountiful resources and its libertarian institutions, is a land that is blessed by God; hence, its citizens possess a unique moral integrity that is tantamount to a spiritual connotation. In place of the outmoded and secularized musical forms, Spitzer informs us that "there exists, for example, in America, the reality of a simple and devout community that is given to express itself in song and mimicry; when this community came to life on the stage in the opera *Porgy and Bess*, with its black, crippled Orpheus as a central figure, and the Negro community as chorus, perhaps a new start was made" (Spitzer, *Classical and Christian Ideas*, p. 124). He also suggests that Marian Anderson's outdoor recital at the Lincoln Memorial on Easter 1939—after the DAR had denied her the use of Washington's Constitution Hall on account of her race—"re-enacted

. . . [for] the 75,000 Americans assembled before the marble steps . . . the idea of the concert of the night sky." Finally, Spitzer lavishes praise on the cinema and its exciting possibilities. Since it is accessible to the masses and combines theater and music, it may "continue the spirit of the opera," especially when the particular film is "in praise of music":

A cinema representing the life of Chopin, or Liszt, or Handel (or Toscanini, not to mention Gershwin and others) is able, thanks to the modern developments of technicolor and sound recording, to offer the masses a fusion of the dramatic, the pictorial, and the musical in which praise of music consists in re-enacting the genesis of given musical compositions or performances, with a historical Orpheus as hero of the photoplay. [Spitzer, *Classical and Christian Ideas*, pp. 225, 125]

Lest it be thought that Spitzer is here echoing Auerbach's theme that social reform and social activism have subverted the role of religious faith in modern society (ancient styles gave way to Christianity, which was itself encompassed by historicism), we must recall that Spitzer, for whom the United States stands as the haven receiving his humanistic faith in Spirit, is attempting to unify his dream of world harmony with his personal responses to American popular culture. The work is confirmed as an "interpretation" that is shaped according to a vision. When Spitzer cites the Marian Anderson concert, for instance, he voids all reference to the political controversy involved—there is no mention of the DAR, Eleanor Roosevelt's supporting role in the procurement of an outdoor stage, or the context of the historical civil rights movement, in which the concert had tremendous significance.[104] Rather, Spitzer depicts the concert according to an ahistorical perspective: as an already confirmed indication of harmony among mankind. From this, from his mawkish (but at the time, fervent) tribute to the American Negro ("a simple and devout community that is given to express itself in song and mimicry"), and from his concern for the masses in the United States, we may well suppose that Spitzer, the man-in-society, on arrival in the United States fresh from the European upheaval, was impressed by the various activist movements devoted to increasing the rights of underprivileged Americans. But instead of reflecting the liberal and radical sentiments that were a part of the reality of these movements, Spitzer, the humanist-detached-from-society, incorporated his perceptions of the American political environment into his larger vision of the United States as the wellspring of an encompassing world harmony based on an abiding faith in the eternal Spirit.

Hence, Spitzer's interest in the possibilities of popular film is based on his belief in the special moral qualities of the American populace. Without this ideal, he might well have held, with Auerbach, that the dissemination of art by mass commercial agencies represented a bleak example of cultural undifferentiation. Spitzer's appeal for (and reenactment of) world harmony culminates in his lyrical vision of the United States as a primary force for the realization of that tranquil and pacific dream; this vision supports his conviction "that the scholar cannot adequately portray what he does not love with all the fibers of his heart." At the same time, he is assured that a prophetic sensibility such as his own is required in order to enlighten the American people about "one of the most heart-inspiring cosmic conceptions ever imagined"—that men might live on this earth in peace and compatibility under the divine patronage of a God in heaven.[105]

In September 1960, Spitzer journeyed to Liège, Belgium, to attend the Congress of the International Federation of Modern Languages and Literatures. His delivery of the concluding paper at the meeting on the study of style aroused the audience to a standing ovation. Following the conference, Spitzer continued on to the Italian resort he frequented at Forte dei Marmi, north of Viareggio. It was there he suffered the heart attack that ended his life. He died on September 16 at the age of seventy-three.

Leo Spitzer's contribution spanned numerous languages, disciplines, cultures, and nations. Since his death, his profound influence on the study of stylistics has repeatedly been acknowledged, but his

159

body of work has had an intimidating effect on subsequent efforts to place him in a historical context. I have attempted to provide a historical context that allows for an approach to Leo Spitzer, in whose fragmented work there is such an emphasis on unity, and who, although combative and argumentative in matters of literary judgment, repeatedly propounds the need for a spiritual concordance among mankind.

If Spitzer's work brings us at times to the point where a mystical leap of faith is required in order to bridge the gap between his revelatory theme and his particular evidence, then it indicates the extent to which his formulation of a critical theory fell short of his vision for that end. But Spitzer always reminded his public that he was human—that he was a man in time striving to achieve a conception of humanity that would transcend all time and temporal existence. In his effort to fulfill his dual task of being a citizen and a prophet, he conceived a body of work that encircles what is mortal and suggests what is eternal; if, in the process, he was subject to human lapses into belligerent polemics and egotism, he did not mean for his vision of a divine order to be tarnished.

Spitzer's persistent refrain of faith and religion provides us with one assessment of the state of our contemporary historical understanding: like a great poem, what we know reflects "the interplay between flowing emotion and restraining intellect."[106] And indeed, Spitzer's literary and historical interpretations exist in that realm, balancing emotion and intellect to attain the magic of a momentary clarity. Since we dwell in a world that mandates both cerebral and intuitive responses to existence, we should be receptive to Spitzer's accomplishment. It does not exist beyond our grasp waiting for the arrival of some momentous insight, it is here, among us, anchored in our lives. And that would undoubtedly please Leo Spitzer. Like Cervantes, on whom he bestowed so much praise throughout his career, Spitzer belongs to "the family of . . . the serene humanists and quiet worshippers of the divine, who saw it in all its variety of earthly forms."[107]

Conclusion

"Historicist humanism," in Auerbach's words, seeks to write "an inner history of mankind"; it features "a conception of man unified in his multiplicity. . . . Ever since Vico and Herder this humanism has been the true purpose of philology: because of this purpose philology became the dominant branch of the humanities."[1] Both Erich Auerbach and Leo Spitzer were descended from this intellectual tradition. They shared a common heritage and discipline. History crossed their lives and prompted them to respond. But their evolutions were not the same.

Auerbach viewed himself as a historical philologist, emphasizing the effect of social forces on literature, the importance of conceptual themes on style. Spitzer thought of himself as a stylistic philologist for whom word and idea were one.

Nowhere is this divergence of approach more evident than in the reaction of each man to the paucity of scholarly materials in the Istanbul library. Spitzer was unable to work and welcomed the opportunity of emigrating to the United States, where improved resources would better allow him to function. Unable to do anything but work, Auerbach produced his mammoth volume, *Mimesis*.[2] Spitzer's procedure—aimed at discerning unities—flourished best among specific texts in the production of particular essays. Auerbach's method—adhering to relativistic fragments—attained fruition in a broad synthesis of historical continuity.

Auerbach's philology sought to disclose "the inner processes of the real, historical world"; his fondness for Vico's association of the historical with the human led him to believe that "whatever we are, we became in history, and only in history can we remain the way we are and develop there from."[3] Literary history is created by the philologist who invests its construction with both his technical skill and personal preferences. The central dilemma of the philologist is to explore the relationship between depicted reality in art and historical reality in life. Such an interaction is intrinsically historicistic and discourages the attainment of absolute truth in favor of relative truths based on historical circumstances. These partial truths are the closest man can come to knowing the "inner processes." History is an authentic force that influences the lives of men and their art.

Philology, to Spitzer, is that discipline which probes the human awareness of what is immortal through the stylistic analysis of words and artistic language. Language represents man's quest to attain the perfect vision of God. The philologist functions in the world as a human being, but he must also detach himself intellectually from the world in order to better comprehend it. The significant area to be examined is the realm of opposition between worldly reality and the world as art perceived from an eternal perspective. It is possible to obtain an intuitive perception of absolute truth provided that the self of the critic is suffused with Spirit and provided that he is guided from the proper point of departure by Providence to the inner essence of life. History is simply the course of ideas as expressed in words.

Both scholars utilized the philological circle as their principal mode of analysis. But Spitzer, whose humanism evolved increasingly toward a mysticism of revelation and insight, insisted on the validity of his method and its click of awareness that dictated both the intention and the critical point of departure. It unified, for him, intuition and analysis. Auerbach, whose radical historical relativism at times allowed for the untempered assertion of popular humanistic values, granted that in practice there are times when the critic's general intention develops as a result of the point of departure.[4] Any method, he felt, must stand in relation to the human philologist who utilizes it at a particular moment in history.

Each man envisioned himself as practicing a humanistic discipline that was solidly grounded in the ways of the world. Since Spitzer believed that words and ideas were inseparable, his response to the oppressive developments of history was to attack the words which had initiated the dubious ideas. Since Auerbach held that literature existed within the world of historical occurrence, his response to the oppressive developments of history was to revise the perceived evolution of literature as a means of altering history.

Thus, their conception of literary history was geared to their individual priorities. Auerbach emphasized the disparity between elitism and the spirit of humanism: humanistic Christianity overthrew the rigid and inflexible ancient separation of styles, but when the religion became a stodgy administrative system of worldly edicts and rules, it was itself overthrown by the spirit of secular humanistic historicism. Spitzer concentrated on the presence of spirituality and humanism in art as manifested by a belief in a world of harmony and perfection beyond the mortal realm. The secularization of the sixteenth and seventeenth centuries served, in his view, to promote the rationalism and positivism that continued to subvert the unified feeling for peace and fellowship on earth and in the world beyond.[5]

Just as their systems of literary history were in contrast, so, often, were their assessments of individual works of literature. Auerbach's Dante was a heroic figure, unique in the history of literature. By writing in the language of his people a work devoted to God, which realistically depicted life on earth, Auerbach believed that Dante had shattered the elitist influence of the Church authorities and had ushered in a more humanistic mode of representation. Dante, to Spitzer, was merely an exemplary genius. He was the model of a man viewing the world with dignity and spiritual grace. To the extent that modern authors emulate this devout poise, they (like Claudel) are carrying on in the tradition of Dante. Auerbach, in search of literary historicism, interpreted Cervantes's energy and enthusiasm in *Don Quixote* as being delightful but whimsical, singular but lacking in substance. He found the novel deficient in romantic humanism and thus considered its world view naive. Spitzer was able to appreciate the greatness of *Don Quixote*. He admired Cervantes's perspectivism for its simultaneous freedom in art and reverence before God—an attitude he found to be appropriate for all time.

Spitzer and Auerbach both labored to produce works of literary criticism for an audience of readers. But their perceptions of that audience did not agree. Spitzer thought of his audience as loyal, omnipresent, and enthusiastic. They constituted an elite: they were the fortunate recipients of revelatory insight from an inspired and prophetic critic. Auerbach had no such certainty about his readers. They were a perplexing quandary. Were they in the United States or in Turkey or in Germany? Would they be able to appreciate the changes in his approach effected by history across time? Ultimately, one worked for oneself out of artistic impulses and trusted that the future would provide the necessary coherence.

Auerbach's was a literary system oriented toward dialectical confrontation. It was particularly well suited to the era of the Second World War, when Western civilization seemed to be on the verge of extinction at the hands of a repugnant fascism. Auerbach's historical humanism flourished during that period; he seized what he regarded as his historical imperative and produced "Figura" and *Mimesis*—two remarkable works of historical criticism—out of opposition to the tenor of the times and in disregard of his own affinity for fragments. But after the war, Auerbach's radical relativism frustrated his ability to adjust to modern society. The cynicism and world-weariness he experienced during his last years were in reaction to his vision of a drab and spiritless present lacking the fire and urgency of historical controversy.

Spitzer's concept of the dissemination of Spirit and the flowering of world harmony could not emerge with any degree of authority during the war. Although he spoke out repeatedly against the forces of totalitarianism, his efforts, concerned as they were with words and derivations, in comparison with Auerbach's, seemed equivocal and tentative. But Spitzer's literary criticism was at home in a world of peace and unity. He was able to embrace the postwar undifferentiation (which so intimidated Auerbach) as an example of the serenity that accompanied a return to the ways of Spirit. Technology and advertising he saluted as the contemporary manifestations of the miracles of Providence. In the process, he helped launch an American school of stylistic literary criticism. Spitzer was dependent on calm and stability for his inspiration, and his last years were positive and exuberant, devoted to his task of personally revealing the encompassing presence of Spirit in our lives.

The careers of Erich Auerbach and Leo Spitzer attest to the arch sovereignty history wields in the creation of literary criticism. Unlike Curtius and Vossler, Auerbach and Spitzer viewed literary criticism as a broad and integrative endeavor that spanned disciplines, professions, and styles of analysis. Both rejected the notion of history as impartial chronicle or unavoidable fate. They opted for a dynamic conception of history as being alive in the minds of men and shaped by the power of their imagination. Hence, the past must be created anew. It must occur and reoccur as a vibrant present in the life and experience of contemporary man. And from out of this reappraisal must emerge the materials with which we live our lives, develop our culture, and shape our own history.

Although Auerbach emphasized the historicistic aspect of literary criticism and Spitzer the stylistic, neither emphasis is sufficient on its own. The formulations of each man reveal the relative strengths and deficiencies of the other. We need the sensibilities of both scholars—the historicistic humanism of Auerbach devoted to the study of man and his literature across a historical evolution of present times; the stylistic spiritualism of Spitzer devoted to the analysis of what is human in art and life across a historical continuum of human visions of the eternal—in order to attain a balanced and working understanding of our own complex and exceptional era.

165

We need their personal "penetration" and their "impartial love" to gauge the "multiple movements" of our literary history. We need to recreate their historical moment within ours. Auerbach's words on Montaigne would certainly have been endorsed by both Auerbach and Spitzer as a statement of their task. Perhaps it is ours, as well: "Is it not great . . . to have taught us how to live on this real earth, without any conditions but those of life?"[6]

Notes

Introduction

1 Erich Auerbach, *Literary Language and Its Public in Late Latin Antiquity and in the Middle Ages*, trans. Ralph Manheim (Princeton: Princeton University Press, 1965), p. 5.

2 Giambattista Vico, *The New Science* (1744), trans. Thomas Goddard Bergin and Max Harold Fisch (Ithaca, N.Y.: Cornell University Press, 1968; reprint ed. 1975), p. 63.

3 Erich Auerbach, "Vico's Contribution to Literary Criticism," in *Gesammelte Aufsätze zur romanischen Philologie* (Bern: Francke Verlag, 1967), pp. 267, 266.

4 Leo Spitzer, "*Geistesgeschichte* vs. History of Ideas as Applied to Hitlerism," *Journal of the History of Ideas* 5, no. 2 (April 1944): 191, 194, 202, 203.

5 Vico, *The New Science*, pp. 415, 414; *The Autobiography of Giambattista Vico*, trans. Max Harold Fisch and Thomas Goddard Bergin (Ithaca, N.Y.: Cornell University Press, 1944), pp. 169, 142, 144, 146; Isaiah Berlin, "Vico's Concept of Knowledge," in *Giambattista Vico: An International Symposium*, ed. Giorgio Tagliacozzo and Hayden White (Baltimore: Johns Hopkins University Press, 1969), p. 375.

6 Ernst Robert Curtius, *Essays on European Literature*, trans. M. Kowal (Princeton: Princeton University Press, 1973), p. xxvi; Ernst Robert Curtius, *European Literature and the Latin Middle*

Ages, trans. W. Trask (Princeton: Princeton University Press, 1953; reprint ed. 1973), p. 588.

7 Curtius, *Essays on European Literature,* p. 293.

8 Benedetto Croce, *History as the Story of Liberty,* trans. S. Sprigge (1941; rpt. Chicago: Regnery, 1970), p. 17.

9 Américo Castro, "Description, Narration and History," (1956), in *An Idea of History,* trans. S. Gilman (Columbus: Ohio State University Press, 1977), p. 304.

10 Leo Spitzer, *Classical and Christian Ideas of World Harmony: Prolegomena to an Interpretation of the Word "Stimmung,"* ed. Anna Granville Hatcher (Baltimore: Johns Hopkins University Press, 1963), p. 198.

11 Erich Auerbach, "Philology and *Weltliteratur*" (1952), trans. Maire and Edward Said, *Centennial Review* 13, no. 1 (Winter 1969): 17.

Erich Auerbach

1 René Wellek, *Discriminations* (New Haven: Yale University Press, 1970), pp. 187, 345.

2 Erich Auerbach, *Literary Language and Its Public in Late Latin Antiquity and in the Middle Ages,* trans. Ralph Manheim (Princeton: Princeton University Press, 1965), pp. 20, 6. "Two recent essays which do seek to evaluate Auerbach's work according to his own estimation of it (but which I encountered only after the completion of this volume) are Thomas M. De Pietro, "Literary Criticism as History: the Example of Auerbach's *Mimesis,*" *CLIO* 8, no. 3 (Spring 1979): 377–87 and W. Wolfgang Holdheim, "Auerbach's *Mimesis:* Aesthetics as Historical Understanding," *CLIO* 10, no. 2 (Winter 1981): 143–54.

3 Ibid., pp. 21, 6–7, 13, 12, 16. Auerbach translated Vico's *Vita Nuova* into German; see note 17. The page numbers cited parenthetically in the text of the discussion of *Literary Language* refer

to the edition cited in note 2, above.

4 Ibid., p. 8.

5 Erich Auerbach, "Vico's Contribution to Literary Criticism," in *Studia philologica et letteraria in honorem L. Spitzer,* ed. A.G. Hatcher and K.L.Selig (Bern: A.Francke, 1958), pp. 31–37.

6 Auerbach, *Literary Language,* p. 19.

7 Ibid., p. 18.

8 Ibid., p. 8.

9 Ibid., pp. 22, 12.

10 Erich Auerbach, *Mimesis: The Representation of Reality in Western Literature,* trans. Willard R. Trask (Princeton: Princeton University Press, 1953), pp. 461–62, 459.

11 Auerbach, *Literary Language,* p. 324. Auerbach here describes Dante as having "the need to dominate life and to impose an order upon it."

12 Yakov Malkiel, "Necrology," *Romance Philology* 11, no. 2 (November 1957): 162.

13 Erich Auerbach, *Die Teilnahme in den Vorarbeiten zu einem neuen Strafgesetzbuch,* Diss. at Heidelberg University (Berlin: Juristische Verlagsbuchhandlung, 1913).

14 Erich Auerbach, *Zur Technik der Frührenaissancenovelle in Italien und Frankreich,* Diss. at Greifswald University (Heidelberg: Carl Winter, 1921).

15 Auerbach acknowledges his philosophical debt to Hegel and the German Romantics in Erich Auerbach, "Epilegomena zu Mimesis," *Romanische Forschungen* 65, nos. 1 and 2 (1954): 1–18. He utilized the influence first in *Dante als Dichter der irdischen Welt* (see note 19, below). Also significant is "The most inspired and influential attempt to apprehend modern history as a whole in terms of laws is dialectical materialism; it grew from the situation in a particular moment of history, and the limits of its validity have now, after a century, become clearly discernible" (Auerbach, *Literary Language,* p. 21).

16 Auerbach, *Literary Language,* p. 16.

17 Giambattista Vico, *Die neue Wissenschaft über die gemeinschaftliche Natur der Völker*, trans. Erich Auerbach (Munich: Allegemeine Verlagsanstalt, 1924).

18 Auerbach, *Mimesis*, p. 189.

19 Erich Auerbach, *Dante als Dichter der irdischen Welt* (Berlin: Walter de Gruyter, 1929).

20 Auerbach, *Mimesis*, p. 194.

21 Otto Friedrich, *Before the Deluge: A Portrait of Berlin in the 1920's* (1972; reprint ed., New York: Avon, 1973), p. 184.

22 George Grosz, *A Little Yes and a Big No*, trans. Lola Sachs Dorin (New York: Dial, 1946).

23 Cardinal Faulhaber, "Judaism, Christianity, and Germany," in *Judaism, Christianity, and Germany: Advent Sermons Preached in St. Michael's, Munich, in 1933*, trans. Rev. George D. Smith (1934), rpt. in *Nazi Culture: Intellectual, Cultural and Social Life in the Third Reich*, ed. George L. Mosse (New York: Grosset and Dunlap, 1966; rpt. 1968), pp. 256–60.

24 Harry Levin, "Two *Romanisten* in America," in *The Intellectual Migration: Europe and America, 1930–1960*, ed. Donald Fleming and Bernard Bailyn (Cambridge: Harvard University Press, 1969), p. 465.

25 Erich Auerbach, "Figura," *Archivum Romanicum* 22 (October–December 1939), pp. 436–89.

26 Erich Auerbach, "Figura," trans. Ralph Manheim in *Scenes from the Drama of European Literature* (Gloucester: Peter Smith, 1973), pp. 71–72. The references cited parenthetically in the text of the discussion of "Figura" refer to the edition cited in note 26, above.

27 Charles Muscatine makes a similar observation (although he uses it to support a point contrary to my position) in his review of *Mimesis, Romance Philology* 9, no. 4 (May 1956), 451.

28 Auerbach, "Figura," in *Scenes*, p. 53.

29 Ibid., p. 41.

30 Ibid., pp. 59–60.

31 Levin, "Two *Romanisten*," p. 465. This information is drawn

from Harry Levin's account of his conversations with Auerbach about Auerbach's residence in Istanbul.

32 This introductory volume, *Introduction aux études de philologie romane*, was written by Auerbach in French during the war. It was then translated into Turkish by Mme Süheyla Bayrav and published in Istanbul in 1944. It was not published in French until 1949 (Frankfort a M.). An abridged version appeared in English, *Introduction to Romance Languages and Literature*, trans. Guy Daniels (New York: Capricorn, 1961).

33 Auerbach, *Mimesis*, p. 556. The references cited parenthetically in the text of the discussion of *Mimesis* refer to the edition cited in note 10.

34 Auerbach, *Mimesis*, p. 18. René Wellek, in his review of *Mimesis*—*Kenyon Review* 16 (Winter 1954): 306—also refers to an existential quality in Auerbach. But his usage points to situations in the literary examples Auerbach provides in which the historical moment closes in on and limits the individual consciousness, thus revealing one's isolation. This is opposed to what Wellek terms the historical situation, when a character's individual nature is incorporated into the larger flow of time and the circumstances of history. Wellek then argues that the "existential" realistic situations in Auerbach contradict the "historicistic" realistic situations, because of their dialectically opposed evolutions from Kierkegaard and Hegel, respectively. This observation, it seems to me, might be valid were Auerbach attempting to formulate a generic theory of realism. But as Wellek admits, he is not. Rather, Auerbach is attempting—through a logical leap that he felt to be imperative and yet remains somehow mystical—to substitute the relative flow of history for the sublime unity of Christianity, as he defined it in figural interpretation. And just as Christ transcended the ancient categories of style by existing among lowly man, so when history bestows contact on lowly man, he is ennobled by the experience, made sublime (and all aristocratic or regimented levels of subject or style are destroyed).

35 Auerbach, *Mimesis*, pp. 201–202.
36 Ibid., pp. 276, 284. Auerbach grants this point in praise of Rabelais's bodily emphasis and its humanistic possibilities; in other aspects he views Rabelais's hedonism as being of ancient or classical derivation.
37 Ibid., pp. 358, 374–75.
38 Ibid., pp. 403, 404.
39 Ibid., p. 491.
40 Ibid., p. 512.
41 This idea was originally expressed by Charles Muscatine in *Romance Philology*, p. 454.
42 Auerbach, *Mimesis*, p. 552.
43 Ibid., pp. 552–53.
44 Erich Auerbach, *Neue Dantestudien* (Istanbul: I. Horoz, 1944).
45 Levin, "Two *Romanisten*," p. 468.
46 For a sampling, see reviews by Ludwig Edelstein, *MLN* 65 (June 1950): 426–31; Helmut A. Hatzfeld, *Romance Philology* 2 (May 1949): 333–38; René Wellek, *Kenyon Review* 16 (Winter 1954): 299–307; Muscatine, *Romance Philology*, pp. 448–57.
47 Ernst Robert Curtius, *Europäische Literatur und lateinisches Mittelalte* (Bern: Francke AG Verlag, 1948).
48 Erich Auerbach, review of *Europäische Literatur* by E.R. Curtius, *MLN* 65 (May 1950): 348–51.
49 Erich Auerbach, "Epilogemena zu *Mimesis*," *Romanische Forschungen* 65, nos. 1 and 2 (1954): 1–18. This article also contains a more extensive critique of E.R. Curtius.
50 Erich Auerbach, *Literatursprache und Publikum in der lateinischen Spätantike und im Mittelalter* (Bern: A. Francke, 1958). See Auerbach, *Literary Language* (the English translation), pp. 22, 24.
51 Ibid., pp. 23–4, 22, 24.
52 Erich Auerbach, "Der Triumph des Bösen, Versuch über Pascals politische Theorie," *Felsefe Arkivi* 1, nos. 2 and 3 (1946), reprinted in Erich Auerbach, *Vier Untersuchungen zur Geschichte der französischen Bildung* (Bern: A. Francke, 1951), pp. 51–74; Erich Au-

erbach, "The Triumph of Evil in Pascal," *Hudson Review* 4 (Spring 1951): 58–79.

53 Erich Auerbach, *Vier Untersuchungen zur Geschichte der französischen Bildung* (Bern: A. Francke, 1951); Erich Auerbach, *Scenes from the Drama of European Literature* (New York: Meridian, 1959). This was the first English edition of the book. It is currently out of print. All of my references labeled Auerbach, *"Scenes"* refer to the 1973 Gloucester edition listed in note 26.

54 Auerbach, *Scenes,* pp. 122–23.

55. Erich Auerbach, "Baudelaires Fleurs du Mal und das Erhabene," in Auerbach, *Vier Untersuchungen,* pp. 107–27; Erich Auerbach, "The Aesthetic Dignity of the 'Fleurs du Mal,' " in *Scenes,* pp. 199–226. An earlier translation appeared in the *Hopkins Review* 4 (Fall 1950): 29–45.

56 Levin, "Two *Romanisten,*" p. 468.

57 Auerbach, *Scenes,* p. 206.

Leo Spitzer

1 René Wellek, *Discriminations: Further Concepts of Criticism* (New Haven: Yale University Press, 1971), p. 189.

2 Ibid., p. 190.

3 Leo Spitzer, *Linguistics and Literary History: Essays in Stylistics* (Princeton: Princeton University Press, 1948; third printing, 1974), pp. 10, 25.

4 Ibid., p. v.

5 Ibid., pp. v–vi.

6 Wellek, *Discriminations,* p. 190.

7 Spitzer, *Linguistics and Literary History,* pp. 18, 10.

8 Ibid., p. 29.

9 Leo Spitzer, "History of Ideas Versus Reading of Poetry," *Southern Review* 6 (Winter 1941): 604.

10 Spitzer, *Linguistics and Literary History,* pp. 38, 7, 9, 19, 35. See.

also Fr. D.E.Schleiermacher, "The Hermeneutics: Outline of the 1819 Lectures," trans. Jan Wojcik and Roland Haas, *New Literary History* 10, no. 1 (Autumn 1978): 1–16.

11 Wellek, *Discriminations,* p. 201.

12 Leo Spitzer, "A New Book on the Art of *The Celestina,*" *Hispanic Review* 25, no. 1 (January 1957): 24.

13 Leo Spitzer, *Classical and Christian Ideas of World Harmony: Prolegomena to an Interpretation of the Word "Stimmung,"* ed. Anna Granville Hatcher (Baltimore: Johns Hopkins University Press, 1963), pp. 149, 128.

14 Ibid., p. 129.

15 Leo Spitzer, "On the Significance of *Don Quijote,*" *MLN* 77 (March 1962): 128.

16 Ibid., p. 115.

17 Spitzer, *Linguistics and Literary History,* pp. 125, 18.

18 Ibid., p. 2.

19 Carl E. Schorske, *Fin-De-Siècle Vienna: Politics and Culture* (New York: Knopf, 1980), p. xviii.

20 Leo Spitzer, "The Mozarabic Lyric and Theodor Frings' Theories," *Comparative Literature* 4, no. 1 (Winter 1952): 13.

21 Allan Janik and Stephen Toulmin, *Wittgenstein's Vienna* (New York: Simon and Schuster, 1973), p. 31.

22 Leo Spitzer, "Interview," *Johns Hopkins Magazine,* (April 1952): 21.

23 Leo Spitzer, "Patterns of Thought and of Etymology: I. Nausea > Of (>Eng.) Noise," *Word* 1, no. 3 (December 1945): 270.

24 Leo Spitzer, "The Formation of the American Humanist," *PMLA* 66, no. 1 (February 1951): 39.

25 Ibid., p. 42.

26 Spitzer, *Linguistics and Literary History*, pp. 2–3, 4.

27 Spitzer, "The Formation of the American Humanist," p. 43.

28 Leo Spitzer, *Die Wortbildung als stilistiches Mittel exemplifiziert an Rabelais.* Nebst einen Anhang über die Wortbildung bei Balzac in seinen "Contes drolatiques" [with a supplement on Balzac's

word formation in his *Droll Stories*] (Halle: N. Niemeyer, 1910).

29 Spitzer, *Linguistics and Literary History*, p. 15.

30 Spitzer, "The Formation of the American Humanist," p. 43.

31 Spitzer, *Linguistics and Literary History*, p. 30.

32 Spitzer, "Interview," pp. 21, 20.

33 Spitzer, *Linguistics and Literary History*, p. 4.

34 Ibid., p. 3.

35 Spitzer, "The Formation of the American Humanist," p. 47.

36 Leo Spitzer, *Die Umschreibungen des Begriffes "Hunger" im Italienischen* (Halle: Karras, Kröber & Nietschmann, 1920). Spitzer provided other accounts of his bureau of censorship experience in "Interview," p. 21; "The Individual Factor in Linguistic Innovations," *Cultura Neolatina* 16 (1956): 83–84; "Why Does Language Change?" *Modern Language Quarterly* 4, no. 4 (December 1943): 424.

37 Spitzer, "Interview," p. 21. The references cited parenthetically in the text of the discussion of Spitzer's life between the wars refer to the edition in note 22.

38 Leo Spitzer, *Essays in Historical Semantics* (1948; rpt. New York: Russell and Russell, 1968), p. 188.

39 Spitzer, *Linguistics and Literary History*, p. 230.

40 Spitzer, "Why Does Language Change?" p. 423.

41 Spitzer, "Interview," p. 27.

42 Leo Spitzer, "The Influence of Hebrew and Vernacular Poetry on the Judeo-Italian Elegy," in *Twelfth-Century Europe and the Foundations of Modern Society*, ed. Marshall Clagett, Gaines Post, and Robert Reynolds (Madison: University of Wisconsin Press, 1961), p. 125.

43 Spitzer, "Interview," p. 27; Wellek, *Discriminations*, p. 188.

44 Spitzer, *Linguistics and Literary History*, p. v.

45 Spitzer dedicated *Linguistics and Literary History* to Professor Hatcher (p. v). Acknowledgments of her influence and references to her articles are scattered throughout his work.

46 Spitzer, "Interview," p. 27.

47 Spitzer, "History of Ideas versus Reading of Poetry," p. 609.

48 Spitzer, *Classical and Christian Ideas*, p. 105.

49 Arnold Schoenberg, "Composition with Twelve Tones" (1941), in Schoenberg, *Style and Idea*, ed. and trans. Dika Newlin (New York: Philosophical Library, 1950), p. 215.

50 Spitzer, *Linguistics and Literary History*, p. 1.

51 Schoenberg, "Composition with Twelve Tones," pp. 214–15.

52 Harry Levin, "Two *Romanisten* in America: Spitzer and Auerbach," in *The Intellectual Migration: Europe and America, 1930–1960*, ed. Donald Fleming and Bernard Bailyn (Cambridge: Harvard University Press, 1969), pp. 472–73.

53 Leo Spitzer, "*Geistesgeschichte* vs. History of Ideas as Applied to Hitlerism," *Journal of the History of Ideas* 5, no. 2 (April 1944): 191–203.

54 Spitzer, "History of Ideas versus Reading of Poetry," p. 608.

55 Ibid., p. 591.

56 Ibid., pp. 595, 602. To further distinguish Spitzer's conception from contemporary views, it should be noted that he clarifies his usage of "self-contained" to mean "without other than aesthetic relevance" rather than "uncommunicative" or "readerless."

57 Spitzer, "*Geistesgeschichte* vs. History of Ideas," pp. 193, 194. The references cited parenthetically in the text of the discussion of "*Geistesgeschichte*" refer to the edition cited in note 53.

58 Ibid., p. 202. For another attempt to affirm the humanistic nature of German language and literature as opposed to the brutal connotations of Hitlerism, see Spitzer and Arno Schirokauer, "German Words, German Personality and Protestantism Again," *Psychiatry* 12, no. 2 (May 1949): 185–87.

59 Leo Spitzer, "Answer to Mr. Bloomfield (*Language* 20.45)," *Language* 20, no. 4 (October–December 1944): 246.

60 Ibid., pp. 245, 249, 248.

61 Note here Wittgenstein's famous pronouncement, "Ethik und Aesthetik sind Eins," *Tractatus* 6. 421; *Notebooks 1914–1916*, p. 77.

62 Ibid., p. 250.

63 Wellek, "Introduction" to Spitzer, *Classical and Christian Ideas*, p. ix.

64 Spitzer, "Answer to Mr. Bloomfield," p. 251.

65 Spitzer, *Linguistics and Literary History*, p. 123.

66 Leo Spitzer, "Correspondence on Robert Hall, 'State of Linguistics: Crisis or Reaction?' " *MLN* 61, no. 7 (November 1946): 502.

67 Spitzer, *Historical Semantics*, p. 5.

68 For some of Spitzer's other word studies, see "Patterns of Thought and of Etymology I.," *Word* 1, no. 3 (December 1945): 260–76; and "Patterns II. Curse," *Word* 2, no. 2 (August 1946): 142–54. Also, *Traditio* 2 (1944): 409–64 and 3 (1945): 307–64, comprise the early form of his study of the word *Stimmung* which appeared as *Classical and Christian Ideas*.

69 Spitzer, *Historical Semantics*, p. 169.

70 Spitzer, *Linguistics and Literary History*, p. 198.

71 Ibid., p. 11.

72 T. S. Eliot, "The Hollow Men," in Eliot, *The Complete Poems and Plays, 1909–1950* (New York: Harcourt, Brace and World, 1971), pp. 58–59.

73 Spitzer, *Linguistics and Literary History*, pp. 47, 41, 50.

74 Leo Spitzer, review of *Style in the French Novel* by Stephen Ullman, *Comparative Literature* 10, no. 4 (Fall 1958): 371.

75 Spitzer, *Linguistics and Literary History*, pp. 135, 151. The references cited parenthetically in the text of the discussions on Diderot and Claudel refer to the edition of *Linguistics* cited in note 3.

76 Leo Spitzer, *A Method of Interpreting Literature* (1949; rpt. New York: Russell and Russell, 1977), pp. 1, 2–3. The references cited parenthetically in the text of the discussion of *A Method* refer to the edition cited here.

77 Spitzer, *A Method of Interpreting Literature*, p. 128.

78 Ibid., p. 130.

79 Spitzer, "Interview," p. 27.

80 Spitzer, *A Method of Interpreting Literature*, p. 131.
81 Ibid., p. 132.
82 René Wellek and Austin Warren, *Theory of Literature* (1949), 3d ed. (New York: Harcourt, Brace and World, 1970).
83 Leo Spitzer, "*Explication de Texte* Applied to Three Great Middle English Poems," *Archivum Linguisticum* 3 (1951), rpt. in Leo Spitzer, *Essays in English and American Literature,* ed. Anna Hatcher (Princeton: Princeton University Press, 1962), pp. 194, 195.
84 Ibid., p. 246.
85 Leo Spitzer, "*Explication de Texte* Applied to Walt Whitman's Poem 'Out of the Cradle Endlessly Rocking,' " *English Literary History* 16 (1949), rpt. in Spitzer, *Essays in English and American Literature,* p. 14.
86 Walt Whitman, *Leaves of Grass* (1855; reprint ed., New York: New American Library, 1958), p. 214.
87 Spitzer, *Essays in English and American Literature*, pp. 32–33, 34.
88 Ibid., p. 34.
89 Spitzer, "The 'Ode on a Grecian Urn'; or, Content vs. Meta-grammar," *Comparative Literature* 7 (1955), rpt. in Spitzer, *Essays in English and American Literature*, pp. 72, 71.
90 Spitzer, *Essays in English and American Literature*, p. 25.
91 Leo Spitzer, "Understanding Milton," *Hopkins Review* 4, no. 4 (1951), rpt. in Spitzer, *Essays in English and American Literature,* p. 116.
92 Spitzer, *Essays in English and American Literature*, p. 218.
93 Spitzer, "The Formation of the American Humanist," p. 48.
94 Ibid., p. 47.
95 Spitzer, "Interview," p. 19.
96 Leo Spitzer, "Language—The Basis of Science, Philosophy and Poetry," in *Studies in Intellectual History*, ed. George Boas (Baltimore: Johns Hopkins University Press, 1953), pp. 77, 82, 83. The references cited parenthetically in the text of the discussion of

"Language—The Basis of Science" refer to the edition cited in this note.

97 Spitzer, "The Influence of Hebrew and Vernacular Poetry," p. 120.

98 Leo Spitzer, "The Works of Rabelais," in *Literary Masterpieces of the Western World,* ed. Francis H. Horn (Baltimore: Johns Hopkins University Press, 1953), pp. 139–40.

99 Leo Spitzer, "The Individual Factor in Linguistic Innovations," *Cultura Neolatina* 16 (1956): 77–78.

100 Leslie A. Fiedler, "McCarthy and the Intellectuals," *Encounter,* August 1954, rpt. in Fiedler, *An End to Innocence* (New York: Stein and Day, 1972), p. 64.

101 Spitzer, "A New Book on the Art of *The Celestina,*" pp. 4–5, 22, 23.

102 Spitzer, *Classical and Christian Ideas,* p. 3.

103 Ibid. See notes 13 and 68. The references cited parenthetically in the text of the discussion of *Classical and Christian Ideas* refer to the edition cited in note 13 above.

104 Compare Spitzer's treatment with the accounts provided in Marion Anderson, *My Lord, What a Morning* (New York: Viking, 1956), pp. 184–92, or Kosti Vehanen, *Marian Anderson: A Portrait* (1941; rpt. Westport, Conn.: Greenwood, 1970), pp. 237–46.

105 Spitzer, *Classical and Christian Ideas,* p. 4.

106 Spitzer, "The Influence of Hebrew and Vernacular Poetry," p. 119.

107 Spitzer, "On the Significance of *Don Quijote,*" p. 129.

Conclusion

1 Erich Auerbach, "Philology and *Weltliteratur,*" (1952), trans. Maire and Edward Said, *Centennial Review* 13, no. 1 (1969): 4.

2 Harry Levin, "Two *Romanisten* in America," in *The Intellectual Migration: Europe and America, 1930–1960,* ed. Donald Fleming

and Bernard Bailyn (Cambridge: Harvard University Press, 1969), pp. 471–72.

3 Auerbach, "Philology and *Weltliteratur*," p. 6.

4 Ibid., p. 14.

5 Leo Spitzer, *Classical and Christian Ideas of World Harmony: Prolegomera to an Interpretation of the Word "Stimmung,"* ed. Anna Granville Hatcher (Baltimore: Johns Hopkins University Press, 1963), p. 138.

6 Erich Auerbach, review of *Montaigne* by Hugo Friedrich *MLN* 66 (Dec. 1951) in *Gesammelte Aufsätze zur romanischen Philologie,* (Bern: Francke Verlag, 1967), pp. 323–24, 325.

Index

Ammianus, 45–47, 79–80

Anderson, Marion, 157–58, 179 n. 104

Arouet, François Marie (Voltaire), 57–58, 130

Aryanization laws, 25, 42–43

Auerbach, Erich, 1–3, 5–7, 11–82, 83, 87, 119, 129–30, 138, 155, 158, 159, 161–66; on Baudelaire, 79–81; on Christianity, 29, 30–33, 36–37, 47–50, 53, 54–55, 78–79; critical method, 11–20; on historicism, 2; on Montaigne, 54, 82, 166; "New Objectivist" concepts in his work, 24–25; on Pascal, 77–79; on philology, 1, 6; on relativism, 12, 14–16, 18–19, 71, 82, 87; on Jean-Paul Sartre, 80; on separation of styles, 21, 36, 70

LIFE: birth, 20; education, 20; military service, 20–21; librarian, 21; translates Vico's *New Science*, 21; University of Marburg appointment, 23, 25; forced resignation, 25; Istanbul State University appointment, 28; in Istanbul, 35–36; emigrates to the United States, 72; Pennsylvania State College appointment, 72; family, 72; Princeton appointment, 73; Yale University appointment, 73; leave of absence to Europe, 81; summer trip to Germany, 81; contribution, 11, 81; death, 11, 81

WORKS: *Dante as the Poet of the Secular World*, 22–23; "Figura," 28–35, 164; *Introduction to Romance Languages and Literature*, 171 n. 32; *Literary Language and Its Structure in Late Latin Antiquity and in the Middle Ages*, 12–19, 76. *Mimesis*: 19, 36–73, 74–77, 81, 161, 164; Marvell, 38; Homer, 38–40, 41–43; Old Testament, 38–40, 41; Petronius, 41–42, 43; Tacitus, 43–44; the ancient world, 44; New Testament, 44–45; Ammianus, 45–47, 79–80; Saint Augustine, 47; Gregory of Tours, 47; figural interpretation, institutionalization of, 48–49; Dante, 49–53; Boccaccio, 52–53; "creaturality," 53; Rabelais, 53–54, 64; Montaigne, 54, 82; figural interpretation, Christian view of, 55; Shakespeare,

55–56; Cervantes, 56; separation of styles (in Louis XIV's France), 57; Prevost (*Manon Lescaut*), 57; Voltaire, 57–58; Gottfried Keller, 58; historicism, 59–60; Balzac, 59–60, 63; Stendhal, 59–60, 63; Flaubert, 60–61; Zola, 61–62, 63; Woolf, 63–64; Saint-Simon, 64; Proust, 64; modernism, 64, 65–67, 70; modernism, emphasis on the random occurrence, 68; on the future, 69–70; critical responses to, 73; Auerbach's reaction to criticism of, 75–76; reviews of, 172 n. 46.
Neue Dantestudien, 72; review of E. R. Curtius's *European Literature and the Latin Middle Ages*, 73–74; *Scenes from the Drama of European Literature*, 78
Augustine, Saint, 33, 47
Automatism, 126

Baltimore, 106
Balzac, Honoré de, 59–60, 63
Baudelaire, Charles, 79–81, 143
Becker, Philipp August, 99
Berlin, 20, 21; during the twenties, 24–25
Berlin, Isaiah, 3
Beyle, Marie Henri (Stendhal), 19, 59–60, 63
Bloomfield, Leonard, 114–16, 126
Boas, George, 148
Boccaccio, Giovanni, 52–53
Bonn, University of, 102–3
Brecht, Bertolt, 24
Burckhardt, Jakob, 2

Calderón de la Barca, Pedro, 96
Castro, Américo, 5

Cervantes, Miguel de, 56, 123–25, 160, 164
Chopin, Frederic, 158
Christianity, 25–29, 30–33, 36–37, 47–50, 53, 54–55, 78–79, 119–20, 144–45, 155, 158, 163, 171 n. 34; and its relationship to nazism, 25–29, 32–33
Claudel, Paul, 105–6, 128–30, 163
Cologne, University of, 103
Communism, 78, 139
"Creaturality," 53
Croce, Benedetto, 5
Curtius, Ernst Robert, 1, 3–5, 11, 73–74, 83, 165; *Deutscher Geist in Gefahr*, 4; *European Literature and the Latin Middle Ages*, 4, 74

Dante Alighieri, 11, 21–24, 24–25, 28, 29, 33, 49–53, 73, 96, 129–30, 150, 163, 169 n. 11; and figural interpretation, 34, 36
Daughters of the American Revolution (DAR), 157–58
De Pietro, Thomas M., 168 n. 2
Dialectical materialism, 169 n. 15
Diderot, Denis, 125–28
Dilthey, Wilhelm, 2, 88
Divine Comedy, The (Dante), 21, 22, 24, 27, 29, 35, 50
Donne, John, 130, 132
Don Quixote (Cervantes), 123, 164

Einstein, Albert, 96, 122, 152
Eliot, T. S., 122–23
Enlightenment, the, 155
Existentialism, 171 n. 34

Fascism. *See* Nazism
Faulhaber, Cardinal, quoted, 26–27, 27–28, 31, 33

Fiedler, Leslie A., quoted, 152, 179 n. 100
Figural interpretation, defined, 30, 30–33, 34, 36, 40, 48–49, 55
Fin de siècle, 85, 95, 143
Flaubert, Gustave, 60–61
Flowers of Evil, The (Baudelaire), 79
Freud, Sigmund, 95, 96, 101, 122, 125

Geist. See Spirit
Geistesgeschichte (history of Spirit), defined, 2–3, 109, 111–13
Gershwin, George, 158
Gide, Andre, 70
Gigli, Beniamino, 127
Gilman, Stephen, 153
Goethe, Johann Wolfgang von, 2, 97, 155
Gregory of Tours, 48
Greifswald University, 20
Grimm, Jacob, 1
Gröber, Gustav, 3, 88
Gropius, Walter, 24
Grosz, George, 24
Gundolf, Friedrich, 109

Handel, George Frederick, 158
Hartlaub, Dr. Gustav, 24
Hatcher, Anna Granville, 107, 175 n. 45
Hegel, Georg Wilhelm Friedrich, 21, 22, 23, 169 n. 15, 171 n. 34
Heidelberg University, 20
Herder, Johann Gottfried von, 1, 2, 161
Hippocrates, 100
Hiss, Alger, 151
Historicism, defined, 2, 59–60, 87, 154, 158, 161, 163, 171 n. 34

History of ideas, 109. *See also Geistesgeschichte*
Hitlerism. *See* Nazism
Holdheim, W. Wolfgang, 168 n. 2
Homer, 38–40, 41–43, 149, 151
Horace, 96
Humanism, 107, 113, 115, 117, 125, 139, 146, 148, 153, 161, 162–63

Istanbul, 28, 35–36, 43, 62, 72, 79, 104–6, 161
Italy, 100–102, 156

Janik, Allan, 96
John, Saint of the Cross, 130, 132
Johns Hopkins University, 106–7, 109
Joyce, James, 70
Judaism, 5, 25–28, 30–33, 35, 96–97, 106, 119–20, 151

Kant, Immanuel, 112
Keller, Gottfried, 58
Kierkegaard, Sören, 171 n. 34

Leipzig, 99
Liége (Belgium), 159
Liszt, Franz, 158
Lovejoy, Arthur, 109, 111–14, 134

McCarthy, Senator Joseph, 152
McCarthyism, 152
Manchester, University of, 104–5
Mann, Thomas, 70
Manon Lescaut (Prevost), 57
Marburg, University of, 23, 25, 103
Marvell, Andrew, 38
Mechanism, 114–16, 126
Mentalism, 114–16
Meyer-Lübke, Wilhelm, 98, 99–100, 117
Milton, John, 108

Modernism, 64, 65–67, 70
Modern Language Association
(MLA), 145
Montaigne, Michel de, 54, 82, 166
Muscatine, Charles, 170 n. 27, 172
n. 41
Musil, Robert, 95
Mussolini, Benito, 127

Nazism, 1, 32, 34, 35, 41, 42–43,
45, 50, 67, 111–13, 115–16, 118,
119, 133, 139, 149, 164; and
Christianity, 25–29, 32–33;
propaganda of, 58
"New Objectivity," the, 24
New Testament, 44
New York, 145

Old Testament, 38–40, 41
Opera, 157, 158

Paris, 99
Pascal, Blaise, 77–78
Pennsylvania State College, 72
Perspectivism, 122–23, 139, 164.
See also Relativism
Petronius Arbiter, 41–42, 43
Philological circle, 88–91, 92, 110,
114, 118, 127, 136, 148, 152
Philology, defined, 1–2, 3, 11–12,
21, 36, 81, 91, 92, 112, 117,
131–32, 133, 140, 145, 149,
154–55, 161, 162–63
Porgy and Bess (Gershwin), 157
Prevost, Abbé, 57
Princeton University, 73
Protestantism, 97
Proust, Marcel, 64, 70

Rabelais, François, 54, 64, 98, 172
n. 36
Racine, Jean Baptiste, 96
Realism, 11–82 passim

Relativism, 7, 12, 13, 14–16, 18–19,
71, 77, 82, 87, 107, 124, 130,
162. *See also* Perspectivism
Rome, 99
Ronsard, Pierre de, 96
Roosevelt, Eleanor, 158
Rosenberg, Ethel, 152
Rosenberg, Julius, 152

Saint-Simon, Comte de, 64
Sartre, Jean-Paul, 80
Schirokauer, Arno, 176 n. 58
Schlegel, August Wilhelm von, 1,
2, 113
Schlegel, Friedrich von, 1, 2, 113
Schleiermacher, Friedrich Daniel
Ernst, 88, 174 n. 10
Schnitzler, Arthur, 95
Schoenberg, Arnold, 95, 108
Schopenhauer, Arthur, 124
Schorske, Carl E., 95
Shakespeare, William, 55–56, 108
Shapiro, Karl, 131
Simmel, Georg, 2
Socrates, 97
Sophocles, 96, 100
Spain, 156
Spirit (*Geist*), 2, 83–160 passim,
162, 164
Spitzer, Leo, 1–3, 5–7, 83–160,
161–66; on America, 107–8,
113, 120, 134–40, 143–44,
145–48, 149, 151–52, 157–59;
on American advertising,
134–40; on the American uni-
versity system, 145–46; au-
tobiographical details in his
writing, 96–97; on Cervantes,
123–25; on Christianity,
144–45; on cinema, 158–59; on
Paul Claudel, 105–6, 128–30;
critical method, 83–94; critical
method, in America, 108,

140–41; on Diderot, 125–28; on *explication de texte*, 141; on *Geistesgeschichte*, 2; on historicism, 87; on humanism, 107; on Italian prisoners of war and the effects of hunger, 100–102; on Judaism, 96–97; language mastery, 86, 99; linguistic word studies, 117–21; 177 n. 68; on opera, 157, 158; on pantheism, 144; on the philological circle, 88–91, 92, 110, 127, 148; on philology, 91, 92, 131–32, 133, 140, 145, 149, 154–55; on poetic ecstasy, 130–34, 140; on Protestantism, 97; on relativism, 124, on Spirit (*Geist*), 2, 83–160 passim, 164; on Richard Wagner, 124, 130, 132–34, 143; on Walt Whitman, 128, 141–44; writing style, 86

LIFE: birth, 94; father, 96–97; mother, 97; education, 97–99; Ph.D. dissertation, 98–99; *Privatdozent* at University of Vienna, 100; military service, 100–102, 175 n. 36; University of Bonn appointment, 102–3; inherits fortune, 103; family, 103; University of Marburg appointment, 103; University of Cologne appointment, 103; compulsory leave of absence, 103–4; University of Istanbul appointment, 104–6; Johns Hopkins University appointment, 106–7; emigrates to the United States, 106; change of nationality, 85; contribution, 159–60; death, 83, 159

WORKS: "Address to the MLA," 145–48: "Answer to Mr. Bloomfield," 114–17; *Classical and Christian Ideas of World Harmony*, 154–59; *Essays on English and American Literature*, 141–45; *Essays in Historical Semantics*, 118–21; "*Geistesgeschichte* vs. History of Ideas as Applied to Hitlerism," 111–13; "History of Ideas Versus Reading of Poetry," 109–11; "Language—The Basis of Science, Philosophy and Poetry," 148–51; *Linguistics and Literary History*, 83–87, 89–91, 94, 105–6, 121–30; *A Method of Interpreting Literature*, 130–40; "A New Book on the Art of *The Celestina*," 152–53

Stendhal. *See* Beyle, Marie Henri

Synchronism, 155

Tacitus, Publius Cornelius, 43–44

"To His Coy Mistress" (Marvell), 38

Toscanini, Arturo, 158

To the Lighthouse (Woolf), 63, 70

Toulmin, Stephen, 96

Tristan and Isolde (Wagner), 132

Troeltsch, Ernst, 2

United Nations, 148

Vico, Giambattista, 2–3, 12, 15, 17, 18, 47, 161; *New Science* in Auerbach translation, 21; theory of knowledge, 14, 23

Vienna, 95, 97, 108, 122

Vienna, University of, 97–98, 100

Voltaire. *See* Arouet, François Marie

Vossler, Karl, 1, 3, 5, 11, 83, 165